NOTES FROM A
FRACTURED
COUNTRY

NOTES FROM A FRACTURED COUNTRY

Selected Journalism

JONNY STEINBERG

JONATHAN BALL PUBLISHERS
Johannesburg & Cape Town

© Jonny Steinberg, 2007

Published in 2007 in paperback by
JONATHAN BALL PUBLISHERS (PTY) LTD
PO Box 33977
Jeppestown
2043

Reprinted 2008
Limited edition printed in 2008
Limited edition printed in 2009

ISBN 978 1 86842 293 7

Cover design by
MR Design, Cape Town
Typesetting and reproduction of text by
Etienne van Duyker, Cape Town
Set in 10.5 on 14 pt ITC New Baskerville
Printed and bound by
CTP Book Printers, Parow, Cape
Limited editions printed by Mega Digital, Cape

Author's Note

First, thanks go to Jonathan Ball; this book was his idea, as was its title. I am grateful to Jane Rogers, who turned the long and motley collection of articles I gave her into something far more elegant; to Jeremy Boraine, director of publishing at Jonathan Ball Publishers, for his consummate professionalism and his warmth; to Francine Blum, in whose safe hands this book went to production; to my agent, Isobel Dixon, who helped plant the seed; and to Peter Bruce for the honour of five uninterrupted years on the opinion pages of *Business Day*, the finest by far in South Africa's English-language press.

Finally, my thanks to those who, out of love, kindness or friendship, uncomplainingly consented to read and comment on drafts of my columns week in and week out: Antony Altbeker, Mark Gevisser, Lomin Saayman, and Carol Steinberg.

Contents

CRIME

POLICE

ABROAD

THE COUNTRYSIDE

Introduction

I once actually succeeded in hiring Jonny Steinberg onto the staff of *Business Day*. It was like having an actual genius in the newsroom. You could walk right up to him and ask him things! It seems like a long time ago.

He was, I think, a sort of crime writer but it didn't work. He soon got tired of the nickel-and-dime nature of a busy newsroom. A little story here and another one there. It can be terribly boring, day in and day out.

Fortunately Jonny hove into view again. I had decided to use our leader pages to host the most exciting writers in the country and he was a key catch. Sadly, I wasn't able to persuade him to write every week. It would be a fortnightly column.

That also proved fortuitous for it enabled Jonny to combine his research, for a book, in Pondoland in the Transkei, with writing the column. His writing from there on HIV/AIDS is arguably the best journalism this country has produced since it became a democracy. What shone through it all was his ability to combine real empathy with profound insight.

Sometimes I read him and wonder why I bother writing at all.

Jonny Steinberg is a gentleman, too, an increasingly rare thing in journalism. That quality and his genius will shine out from every page in this book.

Peter Bruce
Editor
Business Day & *The Weekender*
Johannesburg, 2007

FRACTURED COUNTRY

Bound by the fear of being patronised

27 August 2007

Here is a story about servants and their masters, and about gift horses and their mouths.

The British charity Digital Links recently offered the national education department enough state-of-the-art computers to train every South African high school pupil in computer literacy. In exchange they wanted R50-million, about a tenth of the cost of buying the same computers new.

The national education department said no. According to a *Business Day* report earlier this month, the department 'viewed second-hand computers as inferior and felt Africa was being used as a dumping ground for obsolete technologies'.

The computers in question were neither inferior nor obsolete. They were two- to three-year-old, top-of-the-range products bought for next to nothing from Barclays, Goldman Sachs and others. With South Africa's national education department uninterested, the charity has looked north. Its offer has been accepted by Tanzania, Uganda, Ghana, Ethiopia, and by Kenya, where a quarter of high school pupils now use these computers.

Why were the South African officials so quick to take offence? Why was their instinctive assumption that they were being condescended to?

The roots of these sensitivities are clearly in our white supremacist past. Goldman Sachs's second-hand computers are reminiscent of the threadbare sweater the baas handed down to the house servant. It is no longer good enough for us; you can wear it now. That is, of course, the Mbeki government's abiding fear; that we have been liberated from South African apartheid into a global apartheid; that our continent is a great, yawning receptacle for hand-me-downs; that black South Africans are destined to be house servants forever.

But there is something wrong here. At offer was IT literacy for the young at basement prices, and we said no. The education department became the house servant only because it thought itself the house servant. It denied South African teenagers access to technology because it believed they had been denied that technology. There is a terribly thin line between pride and self-immolation.

If this is indeed true, that at some level the officials who took this decision are unable to free themselves from mental servitude, we would do well to explore who yesterday's masters were.

Yesterday's masters were a pretty insecure bunch themselves. Isolated and scorned, apartheid South Africa's great anxiety was that it would be cast adrift from Western civilisation and forced to fend for itself on a hostile continent. Saddled with this existential fear, it acquired an obsession with technological self-sufficiency. Apartheid's lodestars were Sasol and Armscor. Denied oil, we would make our own from coal; cut off from the arms trade, we would build our own weapons. *'n Boer maak 'n plan*; and in doing so, he showed his middle finger to the world.

It is telling that the superhero of the high apartheid years was Beaufort West's pretty-boy genius, Dr Christiaan Barnard. Stuck down here alone at the tip of this continent, we transplanted a human heart, before anyone else, before even the American superpower, which was about to put a man on the moon. The entire white volk shared in his glory.

These were the masters of old, the masters to whom black South Africans were once servants: isolated, embattled, scared witless that without self-sufficiency they would be doomed. If it is true that some among South Africa's officials cannot shake off the feeling of being servants, these are the masters into whose gaze their eyes are locked. The suspicion of hand-me-down computers comes straight from white South Africa. Being confronted with machines others have made and passed on, we feel instinctively that we are being belittled or tricked; from apartheid we have inherited a fierce technological nativism.

It is the most unfortunate chip to bear on one's shoulder. Everyone who has ever triumphed has done so by making good with hand-me-downs. The grain farming upon which Mesopotamian civilisation was built was borrowed from the farming settlements of western Europe. The Asian Tigers' era of electronic superiority was the fruit of a triumphant borrowing of European and American technology. In the realm of ideas, too, the best have been borrowers. The Edinburgh intellectuals who fathered the Scottish Enlightenment were honing English ideas.

Those who have flourished have been insouciant and clever. They have had the levity and the confidence to turn hand-me-downs into gifts of possibility. I fear the things yesterday's servants have inherited from their erstwhile masters. The brittle pride, the besiegement, the instinctive sense that what comes from abroad is laced with trickery.

The story of a British charity's scorned computers is just a small tale about a moment of bureaucratic silliness. But it is also a story of our times.

At freedom's door, gutted and broken

13 August 2007

As in many other parts of the country, there is a shortage of long-life milk this winter in the old Transkei town of Lusikisiki. It is proving to be something of a catastrophe. Nobody in these parts has laid eyes on a dairy cow in generations and the outlying villages have no electricity and thus no fridges. For many, no long-life milk means no milk.

When a staple suddenly vanishes, people begin telling stories about why. In the villages around Lusikisiki, the tale that quickly spread during the early winter was that black people had chased South Africa's white dairy producers off their farms, taken them over and ruined them. Hence, South Africa no longer produces milk. If things don't come right, the taste of it will become a memory associated with white minority rule.

I have been coming to this town regularly over an 18-month period. Of the many tales I have listened to, this one is perhaps the saddest and most vivid expression of this place's soul that I have ever heard.

Lusikisiki is the sort of place that has always needed to tell stories about faraway events in order to understand itself. It is, on the one hand, very isolated: in its outlying villages there

21

are few newspapers, no televisions, and no middle class with its sense of worldly connectedness. And yet the fate of this place has been intimately connected to global market forces for at least a hundred years. From the first decade of the twentieth century, these villages have shaped their existence around work in the Reef's goldmines. When the global gold trade prospered, Lusikisiki's homesteads shared in the good times. When the gold industry began its rapid decline in the late 1980s, life in these villages began to crumble, a trauma from which they will probably never recover.

A place at once so isolated and yet so exposed to faraway currents inevitably overinterprets the signs that drift in from abroad; things are always invested with too much meaning. When aircraft began flying over Lusikisiki in the 1920s, a movement arose led by a man who claimed to be in celestial contact with black Americans. He prophesied that these Americans, who had come to know and master white technology, would land in aircraft, chase the white people into the sea, and restore to Pondoland its former independence.

During the 1918 flu epidemic, speculation raged in these parts that the plague had been brought by the white authorities. When, at the tail end of the epidemic, health officials began visiting the villages with flu vaccinations kits, rumours circulated that they were coming to kill off those the plague had missed.

No Western technology has ever been neutral here, whether medical or aeronautical. In its collective memory, this place is acutely aware that its engagements with the outside have never been benign, that it has been defeated in its successive encounters with whites, that for the last century it has been fighting a rearguard battle of preservation.

With elegant economy, the story about the shortage of long-life milk absorbs much of this history. The idea of whites being chased off the land is a sweet fantasy the people of these villages have indulged for generations. It is certainly what came to mind when the aircraft flew over in the 1920s. And it has seldom been out of mind since 1960, when the great uprising of the Pondoland peasantry was put down with military force, an event which has come to signify in the district's oral history the moment at which the Mpondo were finally crushed.

So the idea that white dairy farmers have been hounded off their land is no surprise; it is an image with a long pedigree in these parts. But from where does the second half of the tale arise, which says that the blacks who took over the farms have ruined them?

It comes from the fact that these villagers have been gutted over the generations, their self-belief ruined. They once knew themselves as farmers, but they farm no more. Their men once made lives mining gold, but they mine no more. There is an unprecedented epidemic sweeping through these villages, and despite the emergence of new healers and prophets every day, ancient Mpondo cures are unable to stop AIDS. There is a feeling in this place that it has been robbed, not only of its independence and its livelihood, but also of its wisdom.

And so the idea that blacks have taken over farms is immediately attached to the belief that they have ruined those farms. As if freedom has come too late, the people now freed too humiliated, too long ago severed from the art of the possible, to use that freedom well.

Turning a blind eye to the dangers of a Silvio Sexwale

18 June 2007

Ever heard of a man called Tokyo Berlusconi? Or is it Silvio Sexwale? Forgive me: I keep forgetting who's who. And I'm surprised I'm in such sparse company.

Silvio Berlusconi was once just an Italian media baron famous for the naked game shows on his television channels. Then he stood for public office, and he did so like nobody before him. He took out his considerable wallet and, one by one, bought off large chunks of the political process. By the time his first term as prime minister ended, the Italian political scene was divided between those who'd been enriched by him and those who hadn't.

When I say the political scene, I mean all three branches of government. At the end of Berlusconi's first term, 65 parliamentarians were employees or business associates of his. The budget minister, Giulio Tremonti, was his personal tax attorney. Leading members of parliament's justice commission were also Berlusconi's defence attorneys fighting a corruption case that had been brought against him. As for the judiciary, it has never been clear how many judges were beneficiaries of the prime minister's largesse, but you can be sure that the average personal asset value of the Italian judiciary rose considerably in the mid-1990s.

Do you see where I'm going? There are obviously limits to the parallel I am drawing. Berlusconi probably can't even spell Batho Bonke. Although if somebody were to whisper it to him his ears would surely twitch in recognition.

There is a polite silence about this matter, a discreet aversion of the eyes from Sexwale's way of conducting politics. And yet if there was ever a spade that asked to be called by its name it is this one. A man has just thrown his hat into the race for this country's presidency. He has also just given various members of parliament, cabinet ministers, the spouses of cabinet ministers, at least one judge and one public commentator – who knows who else, it isn't all out yet – sizeable nest eggs. Could the character of a Sexwale presidency ever be written out more clearly?

Well, some might argue, South Africa isn't Italy, and the comparison is a silly one. Berlusconi was an antipolitician; he was swept into power by an electorate at its wits' end with a sclerotic establishment. Italian politics was sufficiently hollowed out to entertain a decade of the macabre and the bizarre.

Not so in South Africa, the argument goes. The African National Congress (ANC) is a coalition of powerful, established interests that range across South African society. A presidential hopeful must offer a programme, a style and a vision that speaks to a bewildering array of ears: from organised labour to established business, pockets of power forged in exile and on Robben Island, provincial blocs of party functionaries, the youth league, the women's league, the South African Communist Party. The texture of politics here is too thick, too intricate, for a single billionaire to redesign the landscape with his wallet. As Anthony Butler put it in these pages last Friday: from Sexwale's '"virtual reality" constituency of multimillion-rand share recipients ... we should draw no firm conclusions about real-world political affiliations ...'

Indeed, some say that Batho Bonke is merely a sign of Sexwale's inevitable failure; knowing that he cannot muster a coalition wide enough to carry him into the presidency, he has embarked on the futile course of buying one.

Then there are those who would not like to compare Sexwale with Berlusconi because they hope to God that Sexwale wins. After all, there's a lot to like about him. He is a genuine champion of political diversity. How many other ANC leaders would say publicly, or even believe in secret, that Xolela Mangcu is a good thing? And given that we currently have a president who has spent years in mortal combat against orthodox virology, isn't it refreshing that Sexwale has few intellectual pretensions? Sane, witty, personable, a man comfortable in his own skin and possessed of abundant political skill, a man who enjoys surrounding himself with talent ... We could only do worse.

Yet neither of these reasons is good enough to conceal or wish away the urgency of the question: what sort of polity will we have created when prominent members of all three branches of government and beyond have been made millionaires by the sitting president?

The answer is that we don't know for certain. The

South African polity is indeed irreducible and complex, and it is impossible to say in advance how a future president's largesse will affect governance, the independence of branches of government, the relation between public policy and private interests.

But do we really want to find out? Surely not. Surely this country is difficult enough to govern already without the wild card of a Silvio B?

Belief in an evil mastermind absolves us of responsibility

11 September 2006

In his book, *Witchcraft, Violence and Democracy in South Africa*, the Australian scholar Adam Ashforth writes of living in Soweto in the early 1990s. 'I was struck,' he remarks, 'by a strange paradox in people's attitudes to state power. On the one hand, every encounter with public authorities, from the pass office (until 1986) and the pensions office to the police ... was marked by bureaucratic incompetence and corruption ... Ordinary people had extensive and intimate experience of public authorities' inability to enforce law or perform necessary services and had few illusions about their capacities.

'At the same time, however, everyday conversation conveyed a powerful sense of the government as an evil organising intelligence behind the "System" that was oppressing everyone. When war broke out between township residents and hostel dwellers where I was staying in 1990, no one doubted that the whole conflagration had been "masterminded" by "the government".'

I thought of Ashforth while listening to talk radio in my car last week. The discussion was about Adriaan Vlok washing Frank Chikane's feet. Caller after caller condemned

Vlok's attrition as hollow and offensive. Their complaint against him was very specific: not merely that he had been less than honest to the Truth and Reconciliation Commission, not just that he had failed to disclose all he knew. Their accusation was that he quite literally knew everything; that stored in his head, or in a secret file that he long ago burnt to ash, was a list of every single person ever killed, tortured or maimed before 1994.

'Thousands upon thousands of murders should spill from his lips,' one caller demanded. It was as if apartheid's violence was kept in the top drawer of Vlok's desk, as if he needed only express his wish out loud and it would come true.

This belief floats in its own universe, impervious to history, to empirical evidence, to common sense. For we know as a matter of record that when Sydney Mufamadi and his team arrived at police headquarters in May 1994, they found a sclerotic organisation in an advanced stage of decay. It was capable of great violence, but it had nothing remotely resembling a mastermind.

Pointing this out elicits anger. It is as if one subtracts from the atrociousness of apartheid's atrocities when one points out that they were not all orchestrated from a single office.

It is not Vlok's legacy that worries me: this manner of thinking about the past mirrors a certain structure of thinking about the present and the future. I am currently conducting research on AIDS and AIDS medicine in the Eastern Cape. I am astounded by the number of people I meet who have made sense of the epidemic by conjuring an Adriaan Vlok, a single, concentrated point of vast evil.

I have met several senior government officials, some of them in the health system, who insist that antiretroviral (ARV) drugs were invented to make Africans dependent on Americans.

'Without these drugs,' one of them told me, 'we would deal with this virus with our own inner resources. It would become like flu. If it were not for the drugs, no-one would be dying ten years from now.'

That more than half the ARVs sourced by the national health department are manufactured in South Africa is neither here nor there. The Vlok argument is not of this world; it does its work somewhere else.

Out in the villages, where people are less educated than government officials, Vlok assumes a very different persona. In a shebeen I visit on the old Transkei coast, there is a perennial discussion among the men and women who drink there. The foundation of the discussion, the fact nobody disputes, is that AIDS is deliberately manufactured. The unknown, the question that is debated over and again, is the identity of the manufacturer. Some point to a Malawian sangoma who works in a nearby town. Others to a white doctor with his needle and syringe. Still others say it is bought and sold on a secret market, that any old witch from any old village can obtain it. For the duration of the discussion the drinkers lull themselves into a fantasy; they imagine that the manufacturer is caught and killed, and the virus is no more.

It is a damaging fantasy. If Vlok was responsible for every death before 1994, then the violence of the early 1990s was merely an epiphenomenon of evil, and there are no questions to ask about the connections between then and now. If AIDS is brought upon us by pharmaceutical companies or witches, we need not face up to the hauntingly difficult connections between intimacy and death. We are delivered of responsibility for negotiating our way through a complicated world. We are left unaccountable for the things we do.

To be black, here and now

13 March 2006

I spent municipal election day in a village of some 500 people on the outskirts of the Eastern Cape service centre of Lusikisiki. I have been doing research here since last October, and everyone knows me. Most regard my presence with benign indifference. But on 1 March I was, for the first time, ostracised in ways that were as powerful as they were silent.

Wherever I went people stopped and asked: 'Where are you going to vote?' I replied that my voting district was in Johannesburg, and that I could not vote because I was here. Some nodded politely and moved on. Others could not mask their disdain and stared at me before recomposing themselves. Still others failed to conceal a trace of amusement. But always there was some discomfort. Beneath the polite silence, it was clear that my relationship with the village was being recalibrated. That I was white and not voting, and that they were black and on their way to the school hall to vote, recast the meaning of who I was. People saw me, now, not in relation to this homestead, or that church, but in relation to the political order. A subtle sense of estrangement made its presence felt.

This is not a village democracy has treated especially well. In 1994, African National Congress (ANC) activists came here and said there would be electricity, running water and roads; 12 years have passed and there isn't a soul who fails to remember that these promises were made and broken. The bodies of the dead travel by hearse from the mortuary to the entrance of the village, and are then carried by oxen to their graves. Building materials are borne on people's backs. Water is fetched from the river in 25-litre containers.

True, pension and grant payments have escalated rapidly since the late 1990s, flooding the village with new money, and everyone is aware that this is a result of democracy. But in the 1980s, young men went to work on the mines as a matter of course, and today there is little work for them.

Nor are people here uncynical about politics. The ANC ward councillor for whom everyone will vote is a well-off man in a fully-serviced, brick-and-mortar house some 20 kilometres away. He is, people believe, naive in the ways of village politics, lethargic and self-interested. But there is not a soul here who would shame herself by publicly acknowledging that she will not vote. And voting means voting ANC.

It is a remarkable spectacle to watch. This is a fractured and troubled village. Young men have no work, and many are ungovernable. It is known that on the night after pension day, elderly women should not sleep alone. Several have been held up at gunpoint and robbed in the small hours of the morning. The perpetrators are the grandchildren of their peers, yet they are afraid to name names.

Nor is strife just intergenerational. It is not uncommon for elderly men to accuse elderly women of witchcraft. The enmities are abiding and deep. Yet on 1 March, all of this is put aside. Everyone stands in the queue together outside the school, and everyone votes ANC.

Business Day columnist Steven Friedman remarked in the wake of the municipal election that in South Africa 'party loyalties are an extension of one's identity'. He is spot on. And it is worth examining the flipside of his insight: when people vote, they also suppress important elements of their identities. In the few seconds it takes for the voter to cross his ballot and deposit it in the box, many aspects of his identity vanish: he is not a desperate young man who robs an old woman of her pension; nor is he a patriarch who accuses his neighbour of witchcraft. All the particularities that constitute a community dissolve for that one moment. Everyone is shorn of detail. Everyone is cleanly and simply a black person in early twenty-first-century South Africa. And everyone thus votes, and votes ANC.

What is the content of this clean, shorn identity? I don't yet know the village well enough to say. I suspect it takes the form of a grand narrative, one which includes the Pondoland peasant uprising of 1960, when white people tried to steal land and quelled the ensuing rebellion with machine-gun fire. It includes the release of Mandela, and Oliver Tambo's homecoming to Bizana. And it culminates in the fact that to be black here and now is to vote, and to vote ANC.

More welfare grants would cause some to stop working ... and so?

27 February 2006

It is sad when people try to win a debate by adopting the values of their opponents, for they have given up the very ground on which they stand; they have committed the discursive equivalent of suicide.

I am thinking of the suicide welfare advocates commit when they respond to those who claim that expanding social grants discourages the poor from working. The standard response is denial. On the contrary, welfare advocates claim, inject a steady flow of cash into a destitute community, and the poor will invest it in their own productivity. The more money you inject, the more the poor will work.

This is cloud-cuckoo-land. It is also morally confused. It makes one wonder whether the grants lobby remembers why it became a grants lobby in the first place.

There is little doubt that many people stop working when they get access to grant money. I do not know of any quantitative study in this regard, but I see it with my own eyes wherever I go. In the countryside service centre of Lusikisiki, for instance, spaza shop owners from surrounding villages descend on the town centre every day in taxis and fill them with mealie meal and beer. A distance of about 100 metres separates the taxi rank from the ware-house stores. A group of young men, bluntly known as rickshaws, are hired by the spaza shop owners to ferry heavy bags from the shops to the taxis.

In January I spent a few days with the rickshaws. They formed something of a subculture. All had drifted from their families for one reason or another. Many were HIV positive, had been thrown out of their homes, and had thus lost, among many other things, access to their grand-parents' pensions.

I visited the rickshaws again in early February to find that three of them were gone. I asked what had happened to them. 'Their HIV disability grants came through,' I was told. 'They don't have to work anymore.'

Another story: In mid-2003 I stood outside a massive, Dickensian bakery in Cape Town. It was 6.00 am. A line of several dozen people snaked around the block. Two hefty security guards stood at the factory gates. Their job was to choose the first 20 people in the queue and to keep the rest out. The lucky 20 were to spend the day in the blister-ing heat feeding the bakery's oven.

I returned every day for a week and interviewed every-one waiting outside. Without exception, they were from the Transkei, had come to Cape Town within the last month, and had come alone – no family in the city, no net-works. As with the rickshaws in Lusikisiki, this ghastly little corner of the labour market was reserved for those who would die if they did not work, those who had lost access to grants.

The point is so obvious, it seems futile debating it: if

these people could survive without queuing at 6.00 am to work in a sweltering oven, they wouldn't; if they had access to welfare grants they would be at home.

What would happen if they didn't need to do the work they do? The supply of casual labour would fall, and its cost would thus rise. Spaza-shop customers would pay a little more for their beer, and you and I would pay a little more for supermarket bread. I'd hazard a guess that the price of Free State asparagus and Boland Chardonnay would rise a little too.

It is taboo among the grant lobby to say these things, as if even whispering them might cause the sky to fall on our heads. Yet the proper answer is: so what? To my mind, it will be a good day when chronically ill young men do not need to carry beer on their backs in order to put food in their stomachs. It will be a good day when the hungry no longer need to queue outside an industrial furnace at 6.00 am.

The question of job creation is, understandably, an increasingly desperate one in South Africa. But this should not stop us from thinking clearly. Human well-being cannot be measured by jobs alone. In his book, *The Dirty Work of Democracy*, crime analyst Antony Altbeker points out that the precipitous decline in South Africa's murder rate coincided exactly with steep increases in grant payments. If he is suggesting that grants have done something to mend a broken and unstable world, he is right. And if the price we must pay is a decline in the supply of cheap, nasty labour, then so be it.

Works programmes are not the way out of permanent poverty

31 October 2005

When a commission of inquiry into social security, the Taylor Commission, recommended to cabinet in 2002 that the government institute a basic income grant, the cabinet replied that it would rather get the unemployed working than have them sit at home. The centrepiece of its response was the Expanded Public Works Programme, which it billed as a national project to get the workless into the job market.

In its 2004 election campaign the African National Congress (ANC) touted that the Expanded Public Works Programme would bring large numbers of poor and unskilled people to the labour market: 'a million employment opportunities to be created in the next five years' was its promise. How are we doing on that front?

The programme was officially launched in April, and it is too early directly to measure its impact on poverty and unemployment. But earlier public works projects, upon which the current programme is modelled, have been studied, and it is possible to say with some confidence that the ANC was wrong. The vast majority of those who sign up for temporary employment in the programme will in all likelihood experience 'income shock'. They will spend most of their wage on current consumption. Within a few months, they will be as poor as they were before the programme, and no closer to finding a job.

These findings are extrapolated from an evaluation, written for the UK's Department for International Development (DFID) last December, of the Gundo Lashu road upgrading programme in Limpopo Province.

The irony is that, when measured against sober goals, the Gundo Lashu programme was an overwhelming success. It managed to substitute labour-intensive for capital-intensive construction at no extra cost and with no deterioration in the quality of work. It thus put money in the pockets of very poor people with admirable economy and efficiency. That has to be a good thing.

The problem arises when the programme is touted as something it isn't. For short-term public works employment to take the very poor out of poverty, a delicate balance must be struck. On the one hand, the wage must be low enough for the very poor to select themselves. If the wage is too high, it attracts people already earning income, and draws them out of existing labour markets. Yet if the wage is so low that recipients cannot invest it in schooling, household assets, and productive investment, it will not assist them to climb out of poverty.

The Gundo Lashu experience suggests that demand for unskilled South African labour is so low that this fine balance simply cannot be struck. The wage was too high to attract only the unemployed. And yet it was still too low for significant numbers of people to invest it in their futures. The mean monthly wage for work on the programme was a very modest R579 per month. Even at this low rate, it comfortably beat Limpopo's mean monthly informal sector income, which was R385 a month. It thus came as no surprise that 33% of people who subscribed to the programme gave up other work in order to do so. To attract only the economically inactive, the programme would probably have had to set its mean wage at less than R385 per month.

What did subscribers to the programme manage to do with their R579 per month? The DFID study found that 87% of households with public works employment were living below the poverty line. And 96% of households that had members in public works employment the previous year were below the poverty line. This suggests that, for the three months that people work on the roads, their poverty is alleviated a little. Once the work is done, they revert to their previous condition.

Indeed, the study found that 75% of recipient households did not manage to save money, acquire insurance, or buy assets like cooking implements and furniture. Four out of five households used the wage primarily to buy food, 13% primarily to buy clothes, and 4% to pay for education.

Most concerning of all, perhaps, is that working on the Gundo Lashu programme appeared not to bring people much closer to accessing the open labour market; 19% of former Gundo Lashu employees were working at the time they were interviewed by the DFID researchers, compared to 17% of working-age household members who didn't work on the Gundo Lashu programme. The notion of 'one million job opportunities' rings a little hollow.

So why did the ANC pitch the expanded public works

programme as a job creator? The optimistic answer is that the programme became the victim of over-exuberant election-time spin; that it in fact bears no relation to the serious thinking the ruling party has done about job creation. The pessimistic answer is that it does; that we are truly at a loss when it comes to thinking about employing the unskilled; that we have come to believe in hocus-pocus.

Is your car guard's granny South African?

22 August 2005

In 2003, researchers from the Centre for Social Science Research in Cape Town conducted a census among informal car guards along a one-kilometre stretch of Kloof Street and Long Street in the heart of the inner city. What they found in this eccentric little microcosm tells us a great deal about South Africa as a whole.

The researchers interviewed 53 informal car guards: 17 were South African, while the remaining 36 were from the Democratic Republic of Congo (DRC), Congo-Brazzaville and Angola respectively. Thirty-five of the 36 foreigners were self-reported refugees or asylum seekers.

Among the South African car guards, just under half had no more than a primary school education. Just one in five had a matric. Among the foreigners, in contrast, 40% had some sort of tertiary education, and the majority of the rest had completed high school.

These figures are hardly surprising. Those fleeing places like the DRC who have the means and the aspirations to get as far as South Africa are generally urban, middle-class, and educated. They are abandoning a society in which the conditions of middle-class existence have become precarious or impossible. A recent baseline survey of Congolese refugees in South Africa found that 47% have a tertiary education and a further 33% have matric; 36% were students in the DRC, 20% were skilled professionals, and just 4% were unemployed.

Groomed to take their place among the professional classes of their society, they have had the rug pulled from under their future, and have ended up living in a foreign land where they cannot access credit or open a bank account. In these inhospitable conditions, they negotiate life from the fringes of the urban economy, guarding cars or cutting hair on the pavements.

So, the census findings in regard to education are unsurprising: the road from Kinshasa university student to Kloof Street car guard is not atypical.

Far more interesting is this: during the days, South African and foreign car guards shared the streets, but at night, only the immigrants worked. Why is this? Why did the South African car guards put in seven or eight hours a day, while their foreign counterparts worked the streets around the clock?

I can think of two credible answers. One is that South African car guards are only car guards because they are down-and-outs: dysfunctionals incapable of working much. Foreign car guards, by contrast, are earnest middle-class people who bring their earnest middle-class values of hard work and financial planning to this godforsaken corner of the labour market. This is the view of a Congolese car guard interviewed by the sociologist Owen Sichone.

'South African men will disappear for a whole weekend

and only report back for duty after their money has run out,' the car guard told Sichone. 'They thus do not save and instead live from hand to mouth. They are often surprised to see that foreign Africans who arrive "with nothing", as asylum seekers, soon have more resources than their hosts.' South Africans were shocked, the car guard told Sichone, 'when they found that he lived in a furnished flat and even had a telephone.'

Perhaps there is some truth to this deeply moralistic account, but I doubt it tells the whole story. I suspect the explanation is a good deal simpler. Perhaps foreign car guards work all night because they would starve to death if they didn't. And perhaps the reason they would starve to death is that, unlike their South African counterparts, they do not have grannies who receive state pensions.

I don't have hard evidence for this argument. There is some indirect evidence, though. In 2000, for instance, two Princeton University economists published a study of a sample of South African households which revealed 'a sharp drop in the labour force participation of prime-age men when the elder women of the household reach 60, and the elder men 65, the respective ages of pension eligibility'.

This is a controversial finding, perhaps a shocking and unpalatable one, and a discussion of its full implications is best left for another day. I am not suggesting that young South African men would rather live off their grannies and grandpas than hold down a job. What I am suggesting is that unemployed South Africans who have managed to stay connected to their extended families do not starve to death. They do not have to choose between guarding cars at 2.00 am and hunger.

Perhaps a critical mass of DRC refugees does face that choice. Perhaps that is why the man guiding you out of your parking space after dinner has a foreign accent.

Poor Cape coloureds pay dearly to travel on the road to nowhere

1 September 2003

A current research project has led me to spend time with a poverty-stricken coloured family in Manenberg, Cape Town. Seeing their household from the inside, witnessing the strategic decisions it makes, and the manner in which it negotiates the tortuous geography of the city, is like stepping onto a foreign planet.

The Daniels residence (I have changed the family's name) is home to eight adults and six children. Some of the adults get work from time to time, but for the three months I have known them, everyone has been unemployed. The household's 56-year-old matriarch, Mrs Daniels, sells spices from her veranda every day. By nightfall, she has usually earned enough to put food on the table; on slow days, the family eats bread for dinner. Mr Daniels spends his afternoons smoking Mandrax on the field opposite the house. No-one has the heart to suggest that he quits, or to count what his addiction drains from the household budget.

Mrs Daniels' little business is an intriguing one. The spices she sells are available six kilometres away, at the spice market in Athlone, at prices a good 20% cheaper than hers.

But getting to Athlone from Manenberg costs either a taxi ride or a three-hour return walk, so, by buying from Mrs Daniels, her clients save either money or time.

She has, indeed, found herself an ingenious niche, but she hasn't exploited it. She could, if she played her cards right, become the only quality spice seller on her block, and support her family comfortably off the proceeds.

So why has she not played her cards right? Between savings and loans, she could surely get together the R800 or so required to stock her business properly, to get enough capital to start earning something decent.

The Daniels do indeed save all they can, and borrow more than they should, but the money is seldom invested in Mrs Daniels' business. At first I thought their savings were being eaten up by things like school fees and shoes for the kids: a cycle of recurring but vital expenses. But I soon discovered that this was only part of the truth. Much of the family's meagre savings are burned in an arduous battle against the travesty of Cape Town's urban planning.

The ghettos on the Cape Flats are a perverse parody of the English Garden City. The idea apartheid's planners borrowed, if they ever really believed it, was to take workers and industry to the periphery of the metropolis. The kids would grow up in village-like clusters surrounded by greenbelts, and their parents would find their way to the city on a six-lane super highway.

But the 'cluster' is a claustrophobic, labyrinthine ghetto, the 'greenbelts' are windswept scrublands, and travelling on the highway is exorbitant for the very poor. Much of the Daniels' savings, I discovered, is spent simply on getting out of the ghetto.

Three months ago, their television set broke. There is no television repair shop in the neighbourhood, so they borrowed money for taxi fare to Grassy Park. And when the television did not return, they borrowed more money to go and get it back.

But it is not just necessities like a working television set: the Daniels spend a breathtaking amount of what they have to get out of Manenberg, for whatever reason. It is a point of pride, a matter of human dignity; they need to move through their own city. You witness their anxiety as they squander precious capital for Mrs Daniels' business, but they can't help it.

If you stand on the roof of the Daniels' house you can see the construction work on a new sports facility across the railway track, in the African township of Guguletu. Sometimes the Daniels' neighbours stand on their roofs and hurl racial invective across the track, asking, rhetorically, what has happened to Manenberg's promised sports facilities.

In the living room, Mrs Daniels endlessly plays a tape recording of a local coloured comedian. He talks of sending Mandela back to prison, of how the blacks have stuffed up the government, and Mrs Daniels howls with laughter every time.

It is, of course, deeply unfair. Of the 2 000-odd migrants who arrive in Cape Town every week, most are African and almost all find no work. At least Mrs Daniels knows where to go to borrow R20.

But that is not how things look from Manenberg. The Daniels stew in their misplaced racism, and the old lady's daily earnings will never buy more than dinner and a taxi ride.

Where there is alienation and loss,
American culture fills in

18 March 2003

This column was written on the eve of the invasion of Iraq in late March 2003. Walking through Pollsmoor Prison a couple of weeks before the invasion, I believed I saw here, in a prison on the southern tip of Africa, why the Washington neocons' plans for the Middle East were doomed.

Were you to be blindfolded and led through the corridors of Pollsmoor's maximum security prison, and if you knew the place well, the music in your ears would tell you whose turf you were walking through.

If you detect the sound of West Coast rap somewhere in the din – Snoop Doggy Dog, for instance – you are walking through the 26 gang's turf. If you hear East Coast rap, you are in 28 territory. No 26 member who finds himself in a 28-dominated cell will put Doggy Dog in his ghetto blaster, unless he is looking for trouble.

It's strange, isn't it, that one must go to a prison on the southern tip of Africa to witness American provincialism at its most parochial – Cape Flats men, who will not see Los Angeles as long as they live, defending the city's music with primordial rage.

Take off your blindfold though, and an entirely different America appears. Plastered on the wall in one of the
large communal cells you will see a poster depicting the
Angel of Death draped in the Star-Spangled Banner.
Beneath it, in bold black, a caption: Stop War.

In the cell next door, another poster: here, a giant
American flag fills the scene, and it is dripping in blood.
'Imperialism kills,' reads the caption.

Speak to the inmates and you will find that the people
who stuck the posters on the wall are the very same ones
who declare war by playing Snoop Doggy Dog.

'What do you think of what's happening in Iraq?' I ask.

'America wants to rule the world,' replies an inmate,
who sports a kufiyah on his head.

'After Iraq, they will invade South Africa.'

'Then why do you listen to Doggy Dog?' I ask.

'He's not American, my friend,' the inmate smiles.
'He's universal. I'd die for him.'

What is one to make of this paradox, this simultaneous
love of and hatred for America? Perhaps it is that Snoop
and Tupac are black and defiant, and thus heroes among
heroes, the oppressed lodged in the very heart of the evil
empire.

Or maybe it is just an acute form of intellectual lazi-
ness; maybe America is compartmentalised into two dis-
crete worlds – a cultural paradise and a political hell – as
if there were no connection between them.

I suspect that the paradox is more complicated than
that. I suspect that the hatred grows straight out of the
love, that they are two sides of the same torment.

Sit quietly with a Pollsmoor inmate and ask him what it

means to be a coloured from the Cape, and nine times out of ten the existential anguish pours out in torrents. 'We have no language of our own, no history of our own. We were born when Van Riebeeck screwed his maid,' an inmate told me.

It is especially sad as coloured history is the oldest and among the richest on this subcontinent; the Khoi-San wanderers and herdsmen who invented Afrikaans to communicate with the Dutch; the seers and holy men who came to the Cape from the Dutch East Indies, their presence here evidenced in the shrines that still mark the Peninsula.

All this history was erased and forgotten by generations of poverty and racial exclusion. Today, in the place of historical memory and identity, a thousand tiny American icons stand in. It is no wonder that the love for America is coupled with hate, for the Americanisms are so obviously aped; they are the clutter that fills in a void.

Why should this story of an arcane prison culture in Cape Town have anything to say about the impending war in Iraq? Primarily because Pollsmoor is a microcosm of something much larger.

Everywhere around the globe where people have lost their own histories, or live in a muddled and ambivalent relation to their histories, American culture fills in, half loved, half hated.

The Bush administration believes that the toppling of Iraqi leader Saddam Hussein will trigger democratic revolutions across Arabia and the Middle East, just as Eastern Europe's tyrannies were toppled after the fall of the Berlin Wall.

To believe that – to believe that the presence of the US as invader and as occupying force can be a symbol of freedom – is to misunderstand what America means to the world.

The things that America means are too fraught and painful, too close to histories of denigration and loss.

You can see that thousands of miles from the impending Iraqi conflict, in the corridors of Pollsmoor Prison.

Pollsmoor a ray of hope amid pall of corruption

21 November 2002

In 2001, the president appointed Judge Thabani Jali to head a commission of inquiry into prison corruption. The commission, which had wide powers of investigation and subpoena, sat for more than three years during which it toured the entire country. The spectacles of corruption it uncovered came to constitute an almost daily news diet for South Africans. In late 2002, I sat in the gallery during one of the commission's Cape Town hearings, and was pleasantly surprised by the story that unfolded.

The Jali commission moved its road show to Cape Town last week to hear evidence on corruption at Pollsmoor Prison, and those expecting more of the same were in for a surprise.

Among those who took the stand were former Pollsmoor area manager Fred Engelbrecht and current Pollsmoor admission centre chief Johnny Jansen.

Instead of probing and attacking his witnesses, the commission's chief investigator, Vas Soni, nudged the two men into telling a story. Against all odds, it was a story of redemption; the commission had come to town as the bearer of feel-good news.

The story begins in the late 1980s, when Jansen and Engelbrecht were lowly coloured warders and Pollsmoor was run by a posse of ageing white men. Back then, the prison service was a parody of the nihilism and rot of late apartheid, and Pollsmoor was too bad to be true.

It was the sort of place where prisons service carpets ended up in the living rooms of senior bureaucrats and the engines of state vehicles were converted and installed in private motorboats.

The relationship between warders and inmates was one of warfare. Prisoners would stab warders periodically, and warders would tie prisoners to the bars of their cells and beat them senseless. It was not rare for warders to traverse the prisons with attack dogs and gas canisters.

The relationship between white and coloured warders was one of crass *baasskap*. Jansen recalls a time, in the mid-1980s, when he was called into the office of the head of the prison, which he now occupies, and reprimanded as a 'lying *hotnot*' who was 'rude to baases'. He was told to watch out if he didn't want to have the shit kicked out of him.

In 1989, Jansen and Engelbrecht were among the founder members of the Police and Prisons Civil Rights Union. The formation of Popcru was effectively a declaration of war against the prisons service. For the following five years, the politics of Pollsmoor was honed down to a series of skirmishes between coloured and white warders.

When the African National Congress came to power, the 'lying *hotnots*' took over Pollsmoor; Engelbrecht took up his post in 1996, Jansen took up his in 1997. The old guard cleared out in droves. By the end of Engelbrecht's first year in office, 40 white Pollsmoor managers had left the prison service.

Jansen and Engelbrecht were the bureaucrats now, in charge of one of the most violent and chaotic institutions in the country; between them, they had no managerial experience to speak of. How did they fare?

It would be a lie to say that they performed miracles; Pollsmoor is not a place of miracles. In parts of the admission centre, 55 inmates share a cell which was designed for 18. They share an open toilet and a single basin. Rape is prolific and the prison's thriving drug trade is made possible by corrupt warders.

And yet, Pollsmoor has also moved a million miles in the past few years.

Part of it is captured in numbers: an 80% drop in violent assaults; a 60% drop in staff absenteeism; prison escapes close to zero; prison murders, the bane of Pollsmoor for decades, down to one in the past five years.

After coming to office, Pollsmoor's new management began to initiate a cautious de-escalation of the war between warders and inmates.

In a context where prison gangs sentenced those who communicated with warders to death, management singled out key gang leaders and began talking. The dogs, batons and teargas began to disappear. Managerial action became predictable and rational. The gangs, in turn, began to calm down.

All that had happened, really, was that a group of inexperienced managers began to run the prison with intelligence and with sanity. The result is that the prison has been transformed from an infernal hell into a place of regular human misery.

Why is this story – just a workaday story of a prison being run with a modicum of integrity – worth telling? Primarily because of its contrast with the rest of the prison service.

It is ironic that those who have taken the helm of some of apartheid's most corrupt, decaying institutions have happily inherited the decay; in many prisons in South Africa, the fiefdoms of violence and corruption that reign are indistinguishable from those of a decade ago.

The Pollsmoor story is arresting simply because it is about the curtailment of a long history of sheer madness. It is a shame that the story is unusual enough to bear telling.

CRIME

Looking beyond the easy answers

30 August 2007

Something happened to predatory crime in South Africa earlier this year, something both awful and extraordinary. Having declined during six of the past seven years, car hijacking, cash-in-transit robberies and burglaries surged with little warning in about March-April. Take hijacking, for instance. In the late 1990s, the number of cars hijacked climbed more than 10% a year. The trend suddenly stopped and reversed in 1999-2000. Between then and last year the annual rate of hijackings fell as much as 25%.

Now this year the trend has once again screeched to a halt and reversed. Hollard, one of South Africa's three big short-term insurers, reported that between March and June, hijacking claims soared by 20%. Famously, the police do not release crime statistics often enough for us to know what they know, but authoritative sources at police headquarters say that their figures are similar to Hollard's.

Cash-in-transit robbery figures, which include cross-pavement hold-ups (in which guards are robbed as they carry cash from their vehicles) and some mall robberies, also burst through the roof. At the end of last month they were 33% higher than in the first seven months of 2005.

What is going on? There is talk in senior police ranks about the security workers' strike and about Zimbabwe. The strike, they say, put tens of thousands of embittered, cash-hungry men on the streets, men trained to shoot guns and *au fait* with the criminal networks whose work they are usually paid to thwart.

The argument about Zimbabwe's economic meltdown is similar: a growing surplus on South Africa's streets of jobless, acquisitive men.

The virtue of this argument is its timing. The strike stretched across much of the second quarter of the year, precisely the period during which crime levels rose in earnest. Intuitively, one imagines that so sudden a surge in crime, especially following a long, consistent decline, has a discreet and proximate cause. Something dramatic and unexpected, like tens of thousands of armed and wageless men hitting the streets, seems to fit the bill. But that is where the purchase of the strike argument ends. A sudden surplus of willing hands and feet may explain a surge in crimes such as burglary and the more primitive variants of cross-pavement robberies, but in regard to hijacking and cash-in-transit robbery it leaves too many questions unanswered. These are organised crimes. A hijacked car is stripped and its parts distributed into a network. Or it crosses international borders and enters a transcontinental bazaar. It consists of businesses, organisations, expertise and a network of relationships built over time.

The hijacking industry has never suffered from a deficit of hands and feet. There have always been enough young men prepared to earn a living with a gun.

Something has happened away from the coalface; a market that has been in decline has begun to boom. Why?

For the sake of argument, let us restrict the discussion to hijacking. Perhaps the best way to answer the question is to go back a few years and ask why hijacking suddenly declined about seven years ago. There are probably two answers. One was the introduction of trackers into the South African car market in 1999. The new technology must have taken the hijacking industry off guard. Almost overnight, the odds of finding oneself in possession of a car that would be traced grew from almost nothing to very high.

At much the same time, police investigations of hijacking grew far more sophisticated. Previously, the detective service tackled hijackings in old-fashioned Sherlock Holmes style, one crime at a time, eyes fixed on the scene of the deed.

In the late 1990s, the police, helped by Business Against Crime, assembled hijack-dedicated teams of detectives which began doing things very differently. Instead of understanding the object of their work as a string of incidents and incident scenes, they began to investigate a diffuse network of organisations, people and enterprises. They began to understand hijacking as the beginning of a market chain, and searched for the links most vulnerable to criminal justice intervention.

At the same time, and also at the behest of Business Against Crime, specialist prosecutors began working with detectives and trying their cases in dedicated fast-track courts, raising conviction rates. If all this began to bear fruit seven years ago, why is it not working as well now?

Tracking technology has been effective, but if we have learned anything it is that technological victories in crime fighting do not last forever. Effectiveness ebbs and flows.

The criminal world develops technology-cracking knowledge of its own. There are several tracking technologies on the market, some easier to crack than others. Security personnel are bought off. Criminal enterprises learn over time which segments of the car market under-subscribe to trackers. We are perhaps in a period when the balance in the technology war has shifted.

Regarding the police, several senior officials tell a tale, off the record, of neglect and decline. At the start of their lives, the task teams assembled to tackle hijacking were primed with resources, praise and a sense of importance. Team leaders had their hands shaken and their backs patted by the top brass. If they were short of anything, they could pick up a phone and call a provincial commissioner. They were probably the most inspired and job-satisfied people in the detective service.

After their successes in the early 2000s, the attention and praise began to ebb. Things were going well, so police leaders turned their gaze elsewhere such as aggravated robbery, which was climbing steeply.

Resources were diverted. In September last year the police announced organisational restructuring. An entire tier of the national organisation (area level) was going to disappear. The task teams were located at area level. Suddenly, people were uncertain of their futures.

Their work rate declined. The databases they once used to assemble a portrait of the hijacking industry's market chain began to deplete. Almost by stealth, they returned to the old Sherlock Holmes way – one blind crime scene at a time. It is a classic tale of large bureaucracies. It is never possible to light the whole thing up at once. The fires need to be fed and coaxed all the time.

If there is a refreshing side to the story, it lies in recent police responses to the crisis. No denials, for a start – police managers and politicians have not attempted to conceal the surge in crime. And a will to put things right – it seems there is the sense among senior managers that things have gone awry.

At a broader level, it is perhaps worth noting that too much is often read into rising and falling levels of crime. It is always tempting to view short-term patterns as a barometer of a nation's spirit, a measure of the state of our souls. If hijacking levels fall, there is growing peace in our land. If it rises, we must look for the deep causes of a new wildness.

Sometimes the causes are quite shallow: an effective policing strategy was neglected; a new technology grew a little older.

What murder means for the streets

6 July 2007

This column was published three days after the release of a set of gloomy crime stats for 2006: hijacking, house robbery and business robbery were all up, and murder had increased for the first time in years. I decided to take a longer view and to look at the last decade.

Police leaders across the world have gotten into the habit lately of envying North America. In the last four decades it is the only place on earth to have experienced a dramatic and sustained drop in violent crime. The US murder rate, for instance, declined by almost half between 1992 and 2000 and has remained around 2000 levels ever since. Everybody, of course, wants to know why.

One of the doyens of American crime theory, James Q Wilson, has offered this as a partial explanation: 'As Americans worried more and more about crime,' Wilson wrote in 2002, 'they invested more heavily in self-defense. They moved to the suburbs or to gated communities, bought condos in buildings with armed guards, equipped their cars with alarms and special locks, and avoided dangerous neighborhoods. No one knows how much these changes affected crime rates, but they surely had some influence ... If [a] neighbourhood becomes harder to attack, there will be less crime.'

If Wilson is right about America, then the shadow his observation casts over South Africa is very dark indeed. In the last decade, residents of Johannesburg, Cape Town and Durban have done more than anyone on earth to reshape their cities into postures of self-defence. The gated estates that arise one after the other on the perimeters of our cities; the electrified fences and panic buttons and street booms; the billions of rands invested in private patrols; the Soweto, KwaMashu and Guguletu homes that for the first time sport ten-foot walls and barbed wire tops – nowhere has fear been as powerful a factor in reshaping the cityscape.

And yet if one looks at what has happened to our crime statistics over the last decade, this massive investment in safety is bringing meagre returns. The crimes that the new barricades are meant to ward off have escalated breathtakingly. Eleven years ago, the police recorded just over 77 000 armed robberies per annum. Today, the figure stands at more than 126 000, an increase of almost two-thirds.

In contrast, residential and business burglaries – in which empty homes and businesses are broken into and thus nobody is held up at gunpoint – have declined a little: 319 000 in 1995/6 down to 308 000 in 2006/07. The contrast is ominous. Eleven years ago, for every predator who held someone up at gunpoint, 4.1 empty homes or business were burgled. Today, the ratio has moved to 1:2.4. Wilson says that if you harden targets there will be less crime. In South Africa, it seems, a decade of target hardening has simply spawned a generation of criminals prepared to use more violence. The irony is bitter: an era of fortress building has made us more vulnerable.

This displacement from nonviolent to violent predation as targets harden is vividly apparent in year-on-year comparisons in specific police precincts. Take Parkview in Johannesburg, for instance. Between 2005/06 and 2006/07, residential burglaries declined by 16%. During the same period, residential robbery increased by more than 100%. The shift is stark and obvious.

This burgeoning fashion in armed robbery appears to be reshaping our murder statistics. Between 1995/6 and 2005/06, the annual murder rate dropped by a staggering 31%. In the last year it has increased by 3.6% percent. One year is not nearly long enough to establish a trend, but it is nonetheless worth asking what has happened.

I don't know whether the police have done a thorough study, but on Tuesday, Chris de Kock, the police's chief number-cruncher, reportedly put the increase in murder down to the 26% spike in residential robberies. If he is right, the implications are enormous. It suggests that the burden of murder victimisation is shifting from those who know their killers to those who do not; that fewer people are dying in shebeen fights and neighbourhood disputes, and that more are dying in armed robberies.

That is by far the most significant extrapolation to be made from this year's crimes statistics. It suggests that two simultaneous trends are underway in South Africa. On the one hand, it appears that social bonds continue to strengthen within face-to-face communities, that local mores are taking firmer root. It is difficult to overstate how encouraging that is. Despite great levels of want, despite massive demographic disruptions and the calamity of AIDS, murder statistics tell us that people are managing their relationships with those around them far better than they did a decade ago.

And yet, as hearts grow warmer to those close to home, so homicidal violence against strangers is escalating. What does this say? Essentially that as the transition fades and the shape of post-apartheid society settles, so inequality produces more rancour and resentment. It suggests that our country is becoming increasingly fragmented and parochial: we are, it seems, less a nation than an agglomeration of spiteful, inward-turned villages. It suggests in particular that young men, who are responsible for almost all violent crime, increasingly regard those they know as objects of respect, and those they don't as opportunities for plunder.

What of the future? It takes a fool to forecast crime levels, but being foolish I would hazard a guess that the current escalation of violent predatory crime will not last, simply because South Africans will not tolerate it. The price of bringing crime down, though, will be very dear.

The key, as in so many matters, lies with the mood among the middle classes. The shifting murder trend from familiars to strangers suggests that middle-class people are more likely to be killed by another's hand now than in the past. As tales of violent death spread through middle-class circles, so communities begin to take drastic action.

It is already beginning to happen. In pockets of northeastern Johannesburg, unarmed residents together with heavily armed men are conducting 24-hour saturation patrols, stopping anyone considered suspicious. It is a return to a condition akin to apartheid-era pass laws, but enforced by private citizens rather than the state. As these measures take effect, so crimes like house robbery and hijacking are displaced into neighbouring suburbs, and so neighbouring suburbs are forced to take similar actions. What begins in pockets soon spreads across suburban South Africa, and then extends into poorer neighbourhoods too, as each is forced to defend himself from cascading crime displacement.

If this is right, the rate of armed robbery should gradually decline. James Q Wilson will be proved right after all; he just had no idea how hard targets must get. But the social costs are pretty dismal: entire categories of people excommunicated from public space, not merely because of their skin colour, as in the past, but because they are considered dangerous. And an entire middle class suspended somewhere above the earth in fortified bubbles. It is one thing to feel safer, but at the cost of one's feet never touching the ground?

In the words of a leader who has lost faith – an Afro-pessimist

26 March 2007

President Thabo Mbeki's blog of two Fridays ago – the famous one about the 'kaffir flag' and 'kaffir voting day' – is now ten days old and has been written about widely. But there is something of import that has yet to be said about it, and that warrants saying now.

White South Africa's fear of crime, Mbeki suggested, is a displaced or subterfuge fear of blacks. Centuries of racism have bequeathed to whites a prejudice so visceral and deep that its bearers know not what they do. It is as if whites are culturally programmed to think of a democratic, and thus black-dominated, South Africa as a place of menace and violence.

Mbeki is not wrong. I find myself complicit in prejudice against young black men just about every day of my life. I long ago lost count of the number of white people who send me e-mails in response to something I have written telling me that our country is endemically brutal because it is black. That I am white too means that these things are said matter-of-factly and without shame.

Yet coming from Mbeki, this observation about white racism is not uncomplicated. For he knows better than most that there is a close and dangerous relationship between the humiliation young men suffer and the violence they commit. Indeed, there is a prominent trope in his own public speaking and writing that connects young black men with violence. Speaking, for instance, at the opening of parliament nearly eight years ago, Mbeki invoked 'those in our cities and towns who have ... slid into a twilight world of drug and alcohol abuse, the continuous sexual and physical abuse of women and children, of purposeless wars fought with fists and boots, metal rods, knives and guns, every day resulting in death and grievous bodily harm.'

Reading this passage out of context, one could be forgiven for thinking that Mbeki is citing the words of yet another racist, one who has conjured Africa as a place of relentless sexual violence and murder. But he is quoting nobody. These are his own anguished thoughts.

Another example of the slipperiness of Mbeki's thoughts on white racism and black violence: in his blog two Fridays ago, Mbeki argued that America's penchant for incarcerating blacks en masse was a symptom of white stereotypes of young black men as violent, aggressive, hostile and short-tempered. He cited the Columbia University scholar Manning Marable: 'The driving ideological and cultural force that rationalises and justifies mass incarceration,' Marable writes, 'is the white American public's stereotypical perceptions about race and crime.'

Again, this is not an uncomplicated observation coming from Mbeki, for his government incarcerates young black men for violent crimes at a greater per capita rate

70

than any white government in South Africa's history. On the day South Africa celebrated ten years of freedom, our prisons housed 58% more inmates than they did on the last day of apartheid. This is a staggering figure when one considers that the prison was the abiding emblem of the apartheid era. Moreover, it is hard to find a rational policy imperative behind this hunger to incarcerate. It is difficult not to conclude that what Mbeki's government is expressing towards the young black men in its jails is anger, and perhaps even a sense of betrayal.

Enough examples. The nub of what I am saying is this: when Mbeki came home in 1990 I think what he witnessed horrified him. He believed he had come home to a deracinated and humiliated people. I think he soon came to the view that the most damaged victims of white supremacy were generation upon generation of young black men: men who had, in Mbeki's own words, suffered 'a catastrophic loss of national identity and human dignity', men who had submitted to 'denigration as sub-humans', men who had 'lost all hope and self-worth'.

I think that when Mbeki saw what he did he wondered whether his country's soul had not been torn from its body. And now, nearly 17 years later, he wonders whether the state he governs has the means to heal it. His broadsides against white racism and his penchant for incarcerating black men are, I think, symptoms of the same dispiritedness. They are the thoughts and actions of an odd and unheralded figure – the black Afro-pessimist.

When one looks at institutions like our police force and our health system, when one witnesses their degree of paralysis, one wonders whether one of the maladies from which they are suffering is not the president's disenchantment and his pessimism. Come 2009, I hope we are blessed with a president who still believes in the art of the possible. For I suspect that the one we have now no longer does.

Fleeing the cities we inhabit,
in whichever ways we can afford

26 February 2007

It is no secret that there is an anomaly at the heart of South Africa's current wave of alarm about violent crime. The public outrage is expressed primarily by the middle classes, but the greater share of pain is shouldered by the poor. For those who doubt this, one statistic from a recent South African Police Service study should settle the matter. While one in nine South Africans is white, 32 out of 33 murder victims aren't. Dying by another's hand is not a fate that is equitably shared.

But there is more to the story than numbers. At least as important are the qualitative questions. The most destructive aspect of crime is the fear it instils in us; we shrink from the cities we inhabit, carving out ever-narrower corridors in which we live our lives. The question I wish to ask is: what are the differences between working-class and middle-class corridors of fear? And if we do fear crime differently, what is at stake in the difference?

I had cause to ask myself these questions last month, driving through the empty streets of Johannesburg at 4.00 am with a metered-taxi driver. His name was Nathan. He grew up in a village near Stanger. He came to Johannesburg last year armed with a driver's licence and a family connection at a taxi service. Hence his current job.

I asked him where he stayed when he first moved to the city.

'Right in the middle of Hillbrow,' he replied, 'corner Esselin and Plein Streets.'

'A lively introduction to Johannesburg,' I commented.

'It was terrible. You can't go out at night, not unless you know the Nigerians who run Esselin Street. Otherwise, you can be robbed in a crowded place and everyone will just look the other way. A woman was hijacked right below my window. It was 6.00 pm. The street was full. People turned their heads and kept walking.'

'And the police?' I asked.

He laughed hollowly. 'They are more scared than me. They want to arrest one unarmed man in Hillbrow, he just says no. They have to get backup.'

A month ago, Nathan managed to get out of Hillbrow. He now lives in a garden cottage in the quiet suburb of Kew. 'The only problem,' he remarked, 'is that it is close to Alex. Otherwise it is great. Work in Randburg. Live in Kew. Never see Johannesburg.'

'How did you get the cottage?' I asked.

'I met the people who own the main house at church. They said I could stay rent-free.'

Listening to Nathan, it struck me that the way he dealt with his fear of crime was exactly like, and yet utterly unlike, his middle-class counterparts. They also spend much of their energy sheltering themselves from their city. The difference is that they do so by buying their way into spaces that seem public but are actually privately owned and governed. The office park, the gym, the university, the shopping mall, the gated community.

These are arenas of 'mass private property', as the criminologists Clifford Shearing and Jennifer Wood call them. 'Such spaces,' they write, 'have a strong resonance with medieval common spaces legally controlled by feudal authorities to which certain people had rights of access.'

Nathan couldn't afford to buy his way into these spaces; but what he did do was join an evangelical church. It was a golden investment, for it bought him shelter from the city in the form of a garden cottage in Kew. Of course, that is not all he got out of church; he is no doubt a believing Christian and gets spiritual reward. But I'd imagine that the spiritual and the security rewards are wrapped up together, that separating one from the other is merely an exercise in abstraction. Giving sanctuary from the city's predators is part of what the members of a community of faith do for one another.

Nathan dropped me at the airport, leaving me with an odd thought. If one were to study the lives of the thousands of people who arrive alone in this city every month, would one find that the vast networks of associational life they establish are animated, at least in part, by the quest to be in Johannesburg without living in it? And if this is so, is there not a striking moment of sameness between rich and poor? Some with their wealth, others with their faith, and still others with their ingenuity, the citizens of this city invest considerable resources in fleeing it.

The rich, of course, do better than the poor. The best forms of shelter only money or luck can buy. Hence we close the circle and return to the numbers. Every second South African murder victim, for instance, is unemployed.

The exquisitely intimate fear of villagers

20 September 2006

During the last year, I have divided my time between the middle-class suburbs of Johannesburg, where I live, and a handful of rural villages in the old Transkei. Among the things I have learned is that what criminologists call 'the fear of crime' is as prevalent among Transkei villagers as it is among *Business Day* readers. Crime is spoken of as incessantly, saps as much emotional energy, contributes as much to insomnia. It is perhaps ironic that in a society as deeply divided as ours, the fear of crime is a common thread.

Yet the villager's fear of crime is qualitatively different from the suburbanite's in a way that can be crisply defined: when a villager fears crime she fears people she knows; a suburbanite fears strangers. The difference is enormous.

Take an extreme example. It involves farmers, rather than suburbanites, but the principle is the same. Some six or seven years ago, I was involved in a research project on farm attacks. My research took place along a border: to the east, commercial farmland, to the west, former homeland territory. When the white farmers to the east spoke of crimes committed against them, they told of a racially motivated campaign to drive them from their land; they referred to the criminals as foot soldiers and their shadowy handlers as generals.

In the black villages to the west, middle-class people also spoke incessantly about crime. Priests, nurses, teachers, shopkeepers all talked of how having a car or a good house exposed one to attacks by local thugs. The people who terrorised them were the very same young men who terrorised the farmers on the other side of the road. But of course the shopkeepers and priests did not talk of a political conspiracy to get rid of them. They spoke of this bad egg, and that ruffian, and the family over there that had a wild and unpleasant father.

Two sets of people living a stone's throw from one another, and victimised by the same criminals; yet the respective stories they wove from their fear of crime – about themselves, their neighbours, the future of their country – could not have been more different.

One sees the same thing, albeit less starkly, in Transkei villages. 'As a child,' a villager called Umfundo, who is in his mid-thirties, remarked to me recently, 'whenever I needed to go to town I would get a lift with white tourists. Today, when my son asks tourists for a lift they pretend they have not heard him. I sympathise. They are afraid of the violence of our times. I am afraid of the very same thing.'

He is in fact not afraid of quite the same thing. The tourists are scared of anyone who is young, black, and male. Umfundo is scared of his district's most notorious gangster, who is also his cousin.

It may seem an odd question, but it is impossible to resist: which is more destructive, more corrosive? The suburbanite's fear of strangers, or the villager's fear of people she knows?

At first blush, one may be tempted to conclude that the damage inflicted on the suburbanite is greater. The gap left by the facelessness of one's potential persecutor leaves an awful lot of work to the imagination, and an imagination lit up by fear is no pretty thing. The suburbanite dies a thousand deaths. She chisels out a few narrow corridors through which to traverse her city and live her life. The rest of the world comprises zones of greater or lesser danger. It is surely better to know the object of your fear, for what you know can be delineated, understood and negotiated.

And yet, having spent some time getting to know the fear of crime in Transkei villages, I wonder which is more destructive. To fear being burgled or held up at gunpoint by someone you know, or on the instruction of someone you know, is to be invaded in the most exquisitely intimate fashion. Your perpetrator wants more than your television set or your car. He wants something more personal than that. He envies you, resents you, wants to hurt you. His motives are more complicated and more troubling than those of a stranger.

And your relation to him becomes awfully opaque. Anticipating the crimes of the one you fear, you begin to loathe and resent him as much as you imagine he loathes and resents you, such that the question of who loathes whom becomes difficult and confused.

For a suburbanite, crime is a vividly imagined world of the unknown. For a villager, it is an analogue for the erosion of community. It is spoken of in the same breath as betrayal. It is about estrangement among familiars.

Old hijackers may turn to retail not robbery – given the choice

22 May 2006

The debate about the relationship between crime and unemployment is so old, so tired, so thoroughly battered by cliché, it tends to switch off the brightest minds. But every so often, something unexpectedly fresh appears, something that helps us to think.

In the late 1990s, two American economists published an extraordinary study on the effects of vehicle tracking technology on car theft. They chose six cities which had allowed the introduction of car trackers, and compared them to 44 cities which had not. In the five years preceding the existence of tracking, vehicle thefts per capita in all 50 cities had climbed by about 20%. In the first four years following the introduction of trackers, vehicle theft in the six tracker cities plummeted by 17%: the trend had almost reversed. In the 44 tracker-free cities, levels of vehicle theft did not decline: they stabilised. Clearly, many people who once stole cars in the six tracker cities were now doing something else for a living.

But what, precisely? What did they do instead? The authors asked whether other crimes, like mugging and robbery, increased in the six tracker cities, and found that they had not. They concluded that those who abandoned car theft generally found legitimate work.

In a recently published paper, former Institute for Security Studies analyst Antony Altbeker found that something equally extraordinary happened in South Africa in 1999. In the two preceding years, absolute numbers of car thefts and hijackings rose by 12%. In 1998/99, the trend abruptly stopped and reversed. During the following six years, both crimes dropped by more than 21%.

As in the six US cities, car theft had suddenly become much riskier. The introduction of tracking technology is certainly one reason, as perhaps are other factors such as improvements in the vehicle registration system.

Like his American counterparts, Altbeker asked what those who stopped stealing cars were doing instead. He found that during the very period in which auto-theft and hijacking were dropping, the rate of recorded robbery was rising sharply. Between 1996/7 and 2003/4, recorded robberies consistently rose by more than 10% a year.

Altbeker does not argue that the surge in robbery is accounted for entirely by those who gave up stealing cars. Nationally, he suggests, less than 15% of the observed pattern of increased robbery can be explained by decreased car theft. But that is high enough. It tells us that a significant number of those who stopped stealing cars began mugging and robbing instead. Why in South Africa, but not in the US? Where lies the difference?

One is that American car thieves clearly have less of a taste for violence than their South African counterparts. They are not prepared to substitute sticking guns and knives in people's faces for stealing empty cars. That could mean that they are less hardened than their South African peers. But it could also mean that, unlike South African robbers, they know they face a good chance of being caught. The difference between the two countries could primarily be one of law enforcement capacity; we are simply witnessing a displacement of crime from a strong to a weak area of South African law enforcement.

A related explanation suggests itself. The other day, I found myself reading an American true-crime book. In December 2001, a small-town Oregon man named Chris Longo murdered his family, stole a car, and drove to San Francisco, where he did not know a soul. He slept in the back of his car that night, ate takeouts, and quickly discovered that he had run out of money; he needed a job. The day after arriving in San Francisco, he walked into a Starbucks branch and filled out a job application form. The branch manager accepted his application and told him he'd have work within a few days.

In the event, Longo never took up his Starbucks job; he fled to Mexico instead. But for our purposes, the story offers much insight. Imagine an anonymous South African getting onto a train, travelling across half the country, arriving in a large city alone, walking into a retail outlet, and getting a job. It's unthinkable. It doesn't happen here. And the difference between Longo and my imaginary traveller, I would suggest, goes a long way in explaining the difference between Altbeker's findings and those of his American counterparts.

For somebody looking to leave South Africa's car theft business, getting an honest job is not an easy option, and thus not a sensible choice. Better to scan the law enforcement apparatus for its weakest links.

A story of love and pride,
sons and mothers and armed robbery

27 March 2006

About a month ago, I had the good fortune to interview the most articulate career criminal I have ever met, a genuine organic intellectual of the underworld. His name is Thokozani, he lives with his mother near Port St Johns in the Eastern Cape, and he is facing trial for armed robbery. He is almost certain to be convicted and to spend many years behind bars.

I am sure that much of the story he told me is untrue, but that does not matter: his justification for a life of crime is sophisticated and beguiling; it borrows liberally from a host of ideas you and I cherish.

'I am one of four children,' he told me. 'When we were growing up, my mom worked hard and was poor. You know how it is with poor families: there is not enough money to pay the same attention to everyone. It is not possible for everybody to get school books, and school clothes, and transport money to get to school on time, right up to matric. My mother had to choose.

'Whether she was aware of what she was doing or not, her thinking went like this: "I can't give them all a future, but I can give one of them a future. And then maybe the

83

one who I choose, he will be able to give us all a future. If one of them can get to university, he will save us all."

'So my mother looked on us like we were horses in a race. Her job was to bet on a horse. I was the horse. Why none of the other three? Two are girls, and my brother was a very shy boy. He didn't look like he was going to win the race. So it was me. I was the winning horse.

'I spent a lot of time watching my brother and sisters suffer because I was the horse. I must be the one with dignity, so I must be the one with the best clothes. I must be the one with nourishment for his brain, so I must get the biggest plate of food. I must finish matric, even if the world is about to end. My sisters both left school in standard eight and my mother was pleased because that meant there was more money for me.

'I worked very hard. I was my mother's good horse. I passed matric with a university entrance. I applied for bursaries, and I didn't get any. I had to stay at home. For a year, my mother carried on feeding me, and I choked on the food. I felt I was stealing from my own family. I could have got a job packing bags at the supermarket, but that is not the job of a winning horse. There would have been too much shame.

'So I left home. For six months I avoided my family. When my mother did see me, she cried and shouted. I thought to myself: "I cannot avoid my family. I cannot live like this." So I started coming home with money, money from crime, and I felt like new. I had food for the table. I had school fees for my sister's child. I could breathe for the first time. Whether my mother allowed herself to think about where the money came from is her business. She isn't a fool. She just chose not to think about it.'

'But now you know how it's turned out,' I said, 'that your mother is going to lose you to prison, do you think you did the right thing?'

'I'm like my mom,' he replied. 'I gambled because there was nothing to lose.'

I don't know how much of Thokozani's tale is true. I suspect there was no matric, no university entrance, that things started going awry much sooner. But whatever its relation to reality, the story he has chosen to tell has much power. For it is not a tale of vengeance or destruction. It is about love and pride, about mothers and sons, about the quest to grow into adulthood with dignity.

The chilling heart of Thokozani's tale is this: to be a son, a brother and a man, he claims, he had to give up being a citizen. He held guns in the faces of strangers in order to love and be loved.

The day all South Africa's criminals begin to understand their choices in these terms is a nasty day indeed.

Drug lords had other fish to fry

3 May 2005

A great deal has been written about what the demise of apartheid did to South Africa's licit trade relationships, but very little about what happened to trade in the criminal economy during the same period. The story is fascinating.

We are, it should be said, on speculative turf here. Illicit transactions are by their nature unrecorded, and the instruments that have evolved to measure criminal trade are rough and ready. Some striking developments in the 1990s deserve comment, nonetheless.

The two most dramatic developments were in the export of cannabis to western Europe and of perlemoen to east Asia. In the late 1980s, cannabis exports from South Africa were so negligible they barely registered in European databases. Yet by 1998, British customs had reported that South Africa was the single largest cannabis exporter to the United Kingdom; volumes were estimated to be double those from the UK's previous supply leader, Jamaica. In a decade, the industry had grown from two-bit player to market leader.

As for perlemoen, poaching has existed since seasonal harvesting quotas were introduced in 1970. But in the first 20 years following the introduction of the quotas, poaching volumes were slight. This changed dramatically in the early 1990s. Within a couple of years, the illicit perlemoen trade had become a highly organised, multi-million-dollar industry, controlled by street gangs on the shoreline and by transnational enterprises on the trade routes to east Asia.

By 2002, more perlemoen a year were being confiscated by the authorities than were harvested by the commercial fishery. At much the same time, Hong Kong authorities were reporting that about 1 000 tons of perlemoen a year from southern Africa were being imported, almost three times the size of South Africa's annual quota. With perlemoen selling for as much as $65/kg on the Chinese black market, the value of the illicit industry was in the tens of millions of dollars.

What accounts for this extraordinary growth? One factor was simply the opportunities afforded by the opening of South Africa to the world during apartheid's dying years. Cannabis from South Africa began to be exchanged in a thriving international narcotics bazaar which, by the early 1990s, was several decades old.

Profit margins were so good the wonder is that exporters did not discover the international market earlier. In 2002, for instance, cannabis from South Africa was wholesaling at about $1 350/kg in London, and at $10/kg in South Africa.

In regard to perlemoen, aside from healthy profit margins, a distinctive political factor was at work. In the Western Cape, the coloured coastal working class's relation to the sea is not dissimilar to KwaZulu-Natal peasants' relation to the land. Deep in the annals of coastal communities' folklore and collective memory, harvesting the creatures of the sea is both a survival strategy and a way of life, one that was stolen by government during the apartheid years.

The transition to democracy carried with it a universal expectation that access to the sea ought to open up dramatically. To make the politics of the moment more complicated, many coastal communities expected to be betrayed by the recently unbanned African National Congress.

Political conditions, then, were propitious for illicit harvesting. Entire communities tolerated or turned a blind eye to poaching; in the minds of many, it constituted long-overdue redistribution.

But among the factors that account for this export growth, the decline of the value of the rand from the early 1990s to December 2001 is perhaps the most fascinating. Those who sell illicit dollar-denominated commodities from weak currency zones reap benefits that licit traders seldom can. This is because illicit traders barter. They have done so since time immemorial, and always will.

A trader who brings cannabis from South Africa to an international bazaar can trade his commodity for US dollars and make a handsome profit. But if he is smart, he will trade some of his merchandise for crack cocaine. He will thus have imported crack into South Africa, not by buying it with weak rands, but with dollar-denominated cannabis. Unlike the hapless importers of South Africa's licit economy in the late 1990s, he can skirt the weak currency of his home base whenever he imports.

There is little doubt this practice was, and is, widespread. In the late 1990s and early 2000s, when the prices of imported goods in the licit economy were climbing steadily, the retail prices of imported drugs such as crack and heroin remained stable. It is almost certain that cannabis from South Africa was being bartered for crack and other drugs on a large scale.

Nowhere was the virtuous circle of the barter economy more apparent than in the perlemoen trade. By the late 1990s, much of the Western Cape's poached perlemoen was controlled by Cape Town's prosperous drug lords. Investigators discovered that they were bartering it with Chinese traders for Mandrax, the drug of choice on the Cape Flats.

Everybody made a small fortune. The Chinese bought high-value perlemoen for Mandrax, which they manufactured at low cost. Western Cape gangsters bought high-value Mandrax for perlemoen, which they harvested at low cost. Indeed, by 2000, Mandrax wholesalers on the Cape Flats who bought their commodity in rands could no longer sell at a competitive price. If they wanted to stay in the market, they had to get their hands on perlemoen.

Who benefited from this binge? A handful of people got very rich indeed. Go to coastal villages such as Hawston and Kleinmond and you will see garish double-storey face-bricks standing among the matchbox houses of the working class. Perlemoen money has literally changed the physical landscape.

But there can also be little doubt that its benefits were distributed across a wide spectrum of poor households. Taking perlemoen from the sea without being detected requires employing an army of people in auxiliary functions.

When I visited Hawston in 2002, I was told a story that was no doubt repeated to everyone and may have been apocryphal. 'By 1996, 1997,' several people told me, 'the schools were half-empty. The kids could earn more in a week helping the poachers than their teachers earned in a month. So who wanted to go to school?'

Yet a binge it was. Today, South Africa's stock of wild perlemoen is on the brink of commercial extinction, an accomplishment that has taken the illicit industry little more than a decade to achieve.

This season, poachers have been reported to offer tens of thousands of rands in exchange for being shown untapped banks of perlemoen. In places such as Hawston, which led the binge, there is nothing left at all.

When the history of South Africa's economy of the 1990s is written, I hope a chapter is set aside for the coastal communities along the perlemoen belt, and how their story of boom and bust is so intricately tied to currency fluctuations of which they were only dimly aware.

Some themes in this article are developed in a paper I wrote for the Institute for Security Studies called 'The Illicit Abalone Trade in SA', available at www.issafrica.org

Crime and the shrinking of the future

13 December 2004

Does knowing that he will probably get caught and punished deter a potential criminal from committing a crime?
This is one of the most important questions one can ask
about the criminal justice system. For if the answer is no –
if criminals commit crimes even when they think they will
probably get caught – then one of the primary purposes of
punishment, that of deterrence, is failing.

A related question arises. If the answer is indeed no, if
a criminal isn't thinking about the prospect of being
locked up in prison when he commits a crime, what is he
thinking about? What sorts of emotions, experiences and
feelings are entailed in committing a crime?

Over the last three decades, dozens of social scientists
have tried to answer the question of whether the prospect
of being punished deters potential criminals. Broadly
speaking, they have used two rival methods. The first
begins by convening a focus group of potential offenders.
Each respondent is surveyed for how strongly he believes
he will be caught if he commits certain crimes. The interviewer then places each member of the focus group in a
number of hypothetical situations. For instance, 'Would
you steal $20 in front of a number of witnesses and in the

knowledge that a policeman was in the vicinity?' Or, 'Would you commit date rape if you thought your victim would lay charges against you?'

The results are predictable and encouraging. The stronger one's belief that one will get caught and punished, the less likely one is to say one will commit the hypothetical crime the interviewer has posed. So far so good.

There is a problem with this method though. It does not measure the respondents' actual behaviour, but only how they say they would behave in a hypothetical situation. In other words, the respondents have shown that they are thinking rationally, but do they act rationally?

The second method tries to make up for this weakness in the first. It also begins by convening a focus group and surveying each respondent for how strongly he believes he will be caught and punished if he commits certain crimes. But the second part of the test, the hypothetical situation, is scrapped. Instead, the respondents' actual behaviour is monitored. A year after the focus group is conducted, the subsequent criminal record of each respondent is examined.

The results are much less cheerful. In several studies conducted in the United States in the late 1970s and early 1980s, those who strongly believed that they would get caught seemed just as likely to commit a crime as those who did not think they would get caught.

These results are pretty startling. On the one hand, they suggest that many people who commit crimes just aren't thinking about the future. The fact that they knew they would probably get caught didn't influence their behaviour. But the results are even more disturbing than that. It is not that offenders had consciously decided not think about the future. It's not that they had done a calculation in their minds and decided that committing the crime was worth the high level of risk. For when confronted with an imaginary, pen-and-paper exercise, potential offenders, as the results of the first survey method show, really believe that they will take the future into account when deciding whether to commit a crime.

What accounts for the gap? Why do people think rationally when they are deciding hypothetically, in their imagination, whether to commit a crime, but behave irrationally when confronted with the real, concrete choice of committing a crime in their actual lives?

This is not an easy question to answer. It suggests that committing crime is more about impulsiveness than about rational thought, that crime emerges from a pretty complex range of desires, fears and motives, and that they are powerful enough to shut down thoughts about the future. One is reminded of the formidable tasks facing AIDS education. Does knowing that unsafe sex might kill you prevent you from having unsafe sex? Not always. Not nearly enough. Crime is a bit like unsafe sex. Knowledge drifts into the recesses of the mind. The moment is filled up by a psychological complex in which rational calculation has little place. It surrenders to impulsiveness.

The conclusions are a little dispiriting. The principle of criminal deterrence presupposes that potential criminals are rational beings making calculations about the future. They may be precisely that at most times in their lives, but not when they are committing crimes.

Gangs rule Cape Flats turf with lessons learned behind bars

26 January 2004

It has long become a cliché to point out that the institution of the prison has failed, that it breeds criminals instead of deterring them.

Clichés are corrosive and mind-numbing. They dull the power of the truths they speak – truths that ought to shock us. Every now and again, it is necessary to put the clichés aside and tell the whole story afresh.

For decades now, the street gangs of the Cape Flats have been extorting protection money from neighbourhood shops, demanding a cut of liquor distributors' profits, taking transit fees from the taxis that drive through their turf, maiming those who dare to sell anything without their permission. That is not new.

What is new – about a decade old – is the metaphorical imagination through which street gangsters understand their relationships with those on whom they prey. They have, in essence, taken the imagery and logic of the prison, and imprinted it onto the ghettos.

Take one example: in the Western Cape's prisons, members of the 26, 27 and 28 gangs are called *ndotas*. Every other prisoner is called a *frans*. It has been like that behind bars for nearly a hundred years. A *frans* is a nobody. He has been robbed of the jail equivalent of his juridical personhood. When he receives a parcel from a visitor, he must hand it over to the *ndotas*; they will decide how it is to be distributed. If he wants to conduct a commercial transaction – sell his watch, swap a T-shirt for a toothbrush – he must ask the permission of the *ndotas*. Jail is a strange throwback to the feudal realm: a *frans* rents the very air he breathes.

And so it has come to pass on the streets as well. Since the mid-1990s, the Western Cape's supergangs have come to understand themselves as overlords of a giant prison. The Americans refer to themselves as 26s, The Firm calls itself the 28s. They are the *ndotas*; the taverners, liquor distributors and taxi drivers are the *franse*. They, too, must rent the air they breathe. Cape Town's street gangsters have begun to imagine their neighbourhoods as prisons, each piece of turf a massive jail cell of the initiated, every taxi owner a *frans* to be milked.

That is just one example: it cuts all the way down. Since the mid-1990s, it has become near impossible to scale the ranks of a major street gang without doing time in prison. That is where you learn how to *sabela* – speak prison language; where you learn the difference between a *gazi* – a soldier who is licensed to carry a gun – and a 'silver' – a man of peace, who stores the history and law of the gang in his head.

It is not just the supergangs. The inspiration of prison has permeated the most parochial street corners. In Mitchell's Plain, I met a 21-year-old man who had joined a gang unheard of outside his neighbourhood – the Jolly

Killers. I asked him to do a piece of research work for me and he agreed on condition that I pay a third of his fee in advance. A week later, I phoned him to ask how the work was going.

'I'm not going to do it,' he replied. 'I'm a 26. My work is to con you out of your money.'

'You're a fool,' I said. 'It wasn't much work and if you'd done it you would have earned a whole lot more.'

He laughed patronisingly. 'You don't understand. I'm a 26. That's my ethos.'

'Who made you a 26?' I asked.

'The leader of the Jolly Killers went to jail and became a big 26,' he replied. 'When he got out, he recruited us all.'

Several decades ago, the criminologist Gresham Sykes wrote that 'it is the moral condemnation of the criminal that converts hurt into punishment'. Prison only deters because those who are sent there are stigmatised. He warned, though, that a community can quickly reach saturation point: so many young men go to jail that imprisonment is no longer a stigma, just a well-worn passage into manhood.

Cape Flats street gangs have 'stolen' prison: they have turned the institutions that punish them into fountainheads of inspiration.

It is troubling that this syndrome reached its zenith when it did – on the cusp of apartheid's demise. Scores of youths have greeted democracy by giving it the finger. They have instead embraced an old counter-culture, one which insists that everyone on the planet is either an *ndota*, a *frans* or a cop.

When betraying the dead gives strength to the living

18 August 2003

On a recent trip to the vast, blonde farmlands on the plateau, a farmer's wife told me a tale about the tragic fate of her neighbours.

'He was a gambler,' she began, raising her eyebrows reproachfully, and one would have expected, from these opening lines, a story about a man who had bankrupted his farm, or a husband who had lost his wife to the tractor repair man. She was, in fact, talking about a murder.

'He was a gambler,' she repeated, 'and he only came home at six the following morning. While he was gone, two young black men broke into the farmhouse and murdered his wife. He had gambled away most of his farm by then ...' she continued, and she didn't need to complete her sentence, for it was implicit in the tone of her voice ... and now he has gambled away his wife.

During the last four years, I have spoken to about two dozen people who have lost neighbours to a 'farm attack'. It is extraordinary how often the narrator shapes her narrative into a morality tale, as if the character of the dead person must have had something to do with his murder. It is never enough just to say that fate played a cruel hand, or that we live in a country of much violence. The fragrance of Greek tragedy always lingers about the story, a barely articulated hint that something was awry with this farmer, that family, those people.

This is, of course, nothing new. Doris Lessing's novel, *The Grass is Singing*, published in 1950, contains a chilling account of a remote, white community's response to a 'farm murder': 'The more one thinks about it,' Lessing's narrator writes, 'the more extraordinary the case becomes. Not the murder itself; but the way people think about it … [their] fierce indignation against Mary [the victim] as if she were something unpleasant and unclean, and it served her right to get murdered.'

It is one thing reading of such things in fiction, but quite another to experience it oneself, again and again. Three years ago, I interviewed an elderly couple who had been brutally attacked in their farmhouse a few months earlier. 'Since the attack,' they told me, 'nobody has come to visit. And when we go to town, people we know look the other way. When you catch someone's eye, he greets you briefly because he must; but he does not hang around to chat.'

The psychological wellsprings of this nasty response are fairly clear. Nobody wants something ghastly to happen to them; we all search, instinctively, for a reason why it could never have been us. Blaming the victim, finding something odd or distasteful about him, is a lazy, if effective, strategy of solace.

Yet that is the most obvious and least interesting aspect of the response. More illuminating are all the scraps of superstition and unarticulated belief that clatter noisily in the background.

Take the tale the farmer's wife told me. 'He was a gambler ... That's why he was out when it happened ... He had gambled away most of his farm ...' There are a myriad other salient facts she did not mention. For instance, the deceased's widower was involved in the local commando and it was known that he kept semi-automatic rifles on the property; the perpetrators were probably after guns. It could also be said, and not unreasonably, that his gambling habit saved his life, for he too would surely have been killed if he had been at home.

My interlocutor chose not to talk of these things. Instead, she told the gambling tale. It does not stretch the imagination too far to suggest that the background to her story is this: us whites of the hinterland have lost institutional power and become vulnerable. We have nothing to defend ourselves now but the fibres of our own beings. So we must build those fibres clean and strong. Be good Christians, good fathers, and, above all, good, strong farmers. To fail in any of these tasks is to show a chink in the armour, to make oneself vulnerable: 'He had gambled away his farm ...' and now his wife.

In another place and time, the gambler's story would have been the stuff of tabloid journalism. But the genteel newspapers of the platteland are far too polite to voice such thoughts. Instead, like so much else that rural whites say and think, it circuits the bush telegraph – an isolated community convincing itself that the future will be all right.

Price paid for forgetting the bandits of our past

15 August 2002

Those who attended the opening ceremony at the Sydney Olympics in 2000 were treated to a performance of 50 Ned Kellys dancing to Irish folk music. It is a quirk of Australian national identity that the country has chosen a nineteenth century outlaw as its national hero.

'What is it about we Australians?' asks a character in Peter Carey's novel, *True History of the Kelly Gang*. 'Do we not have a Jefferson, a Disraeli? Might we not find someone better to admire than a horse-thief and a murderer?'

The answer is simple. It is not uncommon for prosperous, relatively egalitarian societies to chide themselves by remembering that they were built on injustice – in Australia's case, on convict labour and genocide. Hence the celebration of an Irish convict's son, a gun-blazing bandit who led a maverick campaign against haughty English landowners.

From a South African vantage point, there is cause to wonder what has happened to our Ned Kellys. For in our own colonial history, there is no shortage of men who robbed in the name of equality and freedom. Where are they now?

I am thinking of one man in particular, whose legacy is so much more impressive than Kelly's, his influence over twentieth century South Africa so disturbing, one needs to ask why he is not a household name.

'Nongoloza' Mathebula was a Zulu migrant who came to Johannesburg in the early 1890s and joined a band of outlaws in the caves of Klipriviersberg south of Johannesburg. A charismatic figure, he soon transformed this motley crew into a tightly disciplined army, its rank structure mimicking the judicial and military hierarchies of the Transvaal Republic. He declared the white state his enemy and infused his army with a crisp political purpose. 'Reading the Bible,' Nongoloza recalled in 1912, 'I came across the state of Nineveh which rebelled against the Lord. I selected this name for my Gang as rebels against the Government's laws.' By 1910, he controlled a quasi-military group of more than a thousand people.

The Ninevites were crushed in a series of skirmishes outside Johannesburg in the mid-1910s. But by then, Nongoloza and his generals had all served time in prisons across northern South Africa and had established their credo wherever they went.

Today's prison gangs, the 26s, 27s and 28s, which control the inmate population in every South African jail, are all descendents of the Ninevites. They maintain the same colonial rank structure established by Nongoloza, their imaginations filled with episodes from early Ninevite history. Their pedigree – consisting of elaborate but imaginary uniforms, a 'law book' of codes and prohibitions, and a language unintelligible to outsiders – has been passed from generation to generation orally and in secret. Most interesting of all is that they have retained Nongoloza's bandit ideology. 'We rob and we steal,' goes one of their mottoes, 'because we have been dispossessed.'

In the past year, I have asked many people about Nongoloza, from Western Cape gangsters to stolen-car runners in Gauteng. Astonishingly, they all tell the identical mythologised history of his life, almost word for word. His legacy has been carefully transmitted through the South African prison system over the course of a century. He is the patron saint of violent criminals.

Why, unlike Ned Kelly, is Nongoloza barely known beyond historians and circles of ex-convicts? For one, he was not nearly as nice as he claimed. Insisting that his enemy was the white state, his most prolific talent was to rob black workers of their wages. He was feared and hated in working-class communities, the sort of man people like to forget.

Second, unlike Australia, South Africa had a proud anticolonial movement, led by refined intellectuals. There was never a need to revere bandits; we had clean heroes. Moreover, anticolonial movements write their own legacies and they tend, understandably enough, to erase people like Nongoloza from history.

So, in one sense, it is fitting that despite his extraordinary legacy, Nongoloza is remembered today primarily by those we despise.

Yet we have also paid a price for forgetting our bandits. Part of the trauma of the current crime wave is that it appeared to come from nowhere, as if it has no antecedents, as if democracy itself gave birth to the things we fear.

Unearthing dead bandits will not make crime go away, but it is nonetheless salutary to understand that we are still living among the debris of our violent and morbid history, that colonialism produced its Nongolozas as well as its Mandelas, its pathologies as well as its heroes. Everything we are experiencing now comes straight from the past.

POLICE

When the prosperous cannot imagine the future

16 July 2007

Nine years ago, when I joined *Business Day* to write about the police, I did what any reporter does and began cultivating informants. Among them were a half-dozen police detectives. I have been meeting each of them two or three times a year ever since.

In the decade that has passed, the life of every one of these men has changed spectacularly, and in each case, as a direct result of the end of apartheid. The new dispensation has made almost all of them considerably wealthier than they could ever have expected to become under the old order.

Take, for instance, a man I shall call Hermann. Born and bred in the northern suburbs of Cape Town, the son of a policeman, he was, when I met him, a 36-year-old detective. He left the police in 2001, following in the footsteps of most of the other white men in his unit.

Nine years later, Hermann runs an upmarket private investigation agency. Most of his clients are large corporations: he catches insurance fraudsters on behalf of financial services providers, gangs of armed robbers on behalf of trucking consortiums, and even a missing deacon on behalf of the Dutch Reformed Church in Bellville he attended as a boy. A generation ago, agencies like Hermann's barely existed; those who wanted to catch runaway deacons and armed robbers generally went to the police.

I saw Hermann a few weeks ago, and we spoke about the public sector strike. 'When I joined the police,' he said, 'it was understood that you can either afford to buy a house or a car. You had to choose. Today, a 25-year-old constable works out that he can't afford both and he has a tantrum. He wants everything, and he wants it now. I sit down in front of the news in the evening, and I cannot relate to the people I see on the screen. Their values, their souls: I feel like I'm watching the news in a foreign country.'

'But Hermann,' I replied, 'isn't it ironic that you now not only have a house and a car, but a swimming pool and a Mercedes? When you joined the police, you expected to spend your working life paying off the bond on a two-bedroom house, retire at 60, and sit out your remaining days on a policeman's pension. And you would have expected the same for your children. They are now probably all going to go to university and will live in a world you once regarded as the stratosphere. All because apartheid ended and you landed with a scarce skill.'

'I never forget that,' he said, 'but who can compare then with now? I have panic buttons in my house. I sleep next to a .45 pistol. This country is not my home anymore, and I am Afrikaans, which means that no other country will ever be my home.'

A few days later, I flipped through the notes from an interview I had conducted with Hermann in 2001, six weeks after he left the police. I had asked him what policing was like in the late 1980s.

'It was horrible,' he answered. 'I was an ordinary detective. The glory boys of the old police were the security branch. Us, we were so under-resourced we kept our vehicles running from the parts of other vehicles. But we had clear tasks. Our commanders had 20, 30 years experience. Our conviction rates were good. You could see the fruit of your labour. Then George Fivaz became commissioner, and that was the end of the detective service. Experienced people left. Commanders became younger and younger; they came straight out of office jobs, didn't know the work. People lost their pride. I came to work every morning feeling hollow.'

There are two stories wrapped together here. One is what has happened to the South African detective service, a terrible tale for another time. The other is a larger story. JM Coetzee once described apartheid as 'nihilistic to its core, a system never intended to achieve more than postpone the inevitable'.

'We can hold the situation for my generation and for my children's generation,' Coetzee quotes a Nationalist politician of the early 1960s. 'And after that, who cares?'

Coetzee is right. The most deeply felt, if seldom expressed, white presupposition of the apartheid era was that the future would always be much briefer than the past; that things were so was a matter of existential certainty. So whether the good fortune the democratic era has heaped upon Hermann lasts one generation or six, it will always be borrowed time. A whole stratum of whites is wrestling with Hermann's paradox: that they are growing more prosperous does not make them any more able to imagine a future.

Forged in South Africa's past, SAPS methods miss the mark

7 May 2007

Would it be fair to describe what the South African Police Service (SAPS) does as old apartheid policing dressed up in new clothes? And if the answer is yes, what turns on it?

At one level, the proposition is obviously preposterous. The SAPS does not demand passbooks from those it encounters on the streets. It no longer has a branch that infiltrates political organisations, and it does not detain political activists without trial. It has also, in the last 13 years, redistributed a significant share of its resources from what was once white South Africa into townships, informal settlements and rural towns.

Yet at a more subtle level, the continuities between the SAPS and its apartheid predecessor are profound. How this came about is perhaps best told as a simple story.

Jackie Selebi arrived at police headquarters in 2000. In his inimitably gruff manner, he demanded of his senior managers that they give him something disarmingly simple: a plan to reduce violent crime.

The police mandarins were pretty excited. For the first time, their boss was a top African National Congress man, someone with clout. He was also clearly a man of action. Back him, and the rewards would be substantial. So the mandarins went away to draft the best crime reduction plan they could think of.

They looked at the organisation at their disposal, and what did they see? It was a 130 000-strong monster, and they had just spent the last six years consolidating it. It was horribly underskilled: for political reasons, it had had to absorb large numbers of incompetent homeland police into its ranks, as well as the *kitskonstabels* the apartheid regime had recruited. The organisation's previous boss, George Fivaz, had famously said that one in four of his cops was functionally illiterate.

So, the mandarins asked themselves, what had this very limited organisation done well over the last six years? The answer was simple: fire fighting. When political conflict saw Richmond go up in flames, a national police task force swooped into the town, saturated it, and restored order. When Cape Town was hit by a series of terror attacks, they did the same on the Cape Flats.

Of course it was something the organisation did well. It required little skill from the troops on the ground; they needed only to be herded into large formations. And saturating places with troops was something lodged firmly in the police's institutional memory, for it is precisely how they policed the townships in the mid-1980s. Indeed, they were old hands.

So the mandarins essentially turned fire fighting into ordinary crime fighting. They put up a map in Selebi's office, showed him the areas of the country hit hardest by crime, and told him they would saturate these areas with patrols, roadblocks and massive search operations. Selebi was pleased, the mandarins were pleased, and the organisation was pleased.

Writ both small and large, that is what the organisation has been doing ever since, over and over again. Ask an average SAPS station commander what he will do if hijacking spikes in his precinct, and he will tell you this: 'I'll plot hijackings on a map, see when and where they occur, increase patrols in that area, put roadblocks around it at strategic times, and do a cordon-and-search operation in the nearest informal settlement in case it has chop-shops.'

If gun crime surges in an area, ask the local station commander what he'll do, and he will say: 'Plot the crimes on a map, see when they occur, and pay lots of cops overtime to go in at the right time and do stops-and-searches'.

This is the stuff that makes the SAPS feel comfortable. It isn't difficult. They've been doing it since the apartheid years, and it's a lot better than doing nothing.

The problem is that it is not very effective at reducing crime, not all crime at any rate. It is good for tackling crimes like street muggings: these are always concentrated into specific times and places, and so well placed saturation policing deals with them very well. But hijackings, house robberies, business robberies – precisely the sorts of crimes that began to surge a year ago – these are too spread out over space and time for large formations of cops to do much about. Policing them requires attention to fine detail, a habit of problem solving, a uniformed service that coordinates its work with that of detectives.

In short, the SAPS does much of what it does because it knows it can, not because it is the most effective way to reduce crime. And it knows it can because it is something it's been doing since the apartheid years.

Is the tale of the SAPS an analogue for a broader governance problem in South Africa?

Where police are petulant and others do their work for them

23 April 2007

Some weeks back, I travelled to a town in the old Transkei to interview a man about his work. I called him on his cellphone when I arrived, and he told me to meet him at the magistrate's court. I could barely hear him speak; he had to shout above the noise of what sounded like an angry crowd.

When I arrived at the court buildings, the grounds were jam-packed with several hundred toyi-toying people. Inside the court, a bailing hearing for five young men charged with murder was about to commence. The person they were accused of killing was a well-known man from an outlying village. He was a successful shopkeeper, a prominent member of his local African National Congress branch, and had attained wide fame on the town's soccer fields as a talented striker.

A week earlier, as he was cashing up in the late afternoon, five young men scaled his fence, shot him dead and ran off with the day's takings.

I spoke to about a dozen people outside the courtroom. Few of them distinguished between a bail hearing and a trial. The way they saw it, these five boys had murdered a beloved man, their lawyers were trying to release them, and the magistrate was going to determine their fate. If they walked free it would be scandalous. But their anger at the prospect of failed justice merged with a far hotter anger: it concerned the conduct of the police.

'The cops were obviously called on the day of the murder,' explained the man I had come to see when I finally found him. 'They set about looking for the killers. One day passed, no arrests. Then another. On the third day, the community called a meeting. It was decided several men would be appointed to find the killers themselves.'

A village is not a difficult place to find the perpetrators of a killing. Within hours, the men appointed by the community had rounded up five youths. They were delivered to the charge office at the local police station, their hands bound with rope. Which is how it came to be that they stood together in the accused box on the day I came to town.

Now, the police had sent word to community leaders that they were going to arrest the men who found and delivered the murder suspects on kidnapping charges.

'That is why there are so many people here,' my companion explained. 'They want to show the police that they are angry, that they cannot arrest the ones who were doing their job for them.'

We filed into the courtroom and sat there jammed together for a long time. The case could not proceed because the investigating officer had failed to turn up to give evidence. We waited and waited. The police station was just a couple of hundred metres up the road. Finally, the magistrate suggested that the detective be called, and that court reconvene in 90 minutes.

We all assembled again an hour and a half later, but the

investigating officer still wasn't there, and the bail hearing was postponed for two days. He, and quite possibly his commanding officer too, had clearly decided to express petulance: this is your case, not ours, and so we'll obstruct where we can.

As we were walking out of court, two grumpy uniformed cops grabbed two youngsters from the gallery, berated them for not dressing smartly for court, pushed them roughly against a wall, and body-searched them. People in the crowd clucked their tongues and murmured in disapproval.

Reflecting on the day's experience, the first thought that came to mind is that old habits die much harder than we think. Back in the days of the old Transkei, when the place was run by a tin-pot dictator, the homeland police was notorious for its arbitrary violence. Talking to people over the last 18 months, I have heard countless stories of men picked up in their villages and thrown in jail for a year without trial or even an intelligible explanation.

We live in a democracy now, and its citizens require a police force that solves crimes. This particular police station clearly can't. What we witnessed in court was its bitter response to its own incompetence. If we are not up to participating in this process, the police seemed to be saying, we will disavow and disrupt it. Which is how they came to find comfort in their old homeland DNA.

I am left with two questions. Will this community ever again report a serious crime to the police? And how has the police leadership of 2007 allowed one of its stations to drift back two decades into the old Transkei?

South African leaders need to snap out of their depression, and govern

12 February 2007

Few dispute that the government is doing an inadequate job, not only in reducing violent crime, but in moderating public fear of crime. With every public appearance our national police commissioner makes, his stubborn, short-tempered defensiveness leaves most of us more fearful and dispirited than we were when he kept quiet. That is a damning indictment if there ever was one.

What should the government be doing to manage public fear, and why aren't they doing it? These are not technocratic or managerial questions. They speak to existential matters, to our government's deepest fears about the nation it has inherited.

Here's what I think a skilled manager of public fear would have done. Last April, when the monthly crime stats hit his desk, he would have been rattled. After years of steady decrease, a number of violent crimes had surged without warning. All were crimes that scare the living day-lights out of the middle class: hijackings, house robberies, robberies at retail centres, cross-pavement cash-in-transit robberies – the sorts of crimes that make a suburbanite feel she is living in a very unsafe place.

Being wise and well informed, our skilled fear-manager would have known that no police force on earth has ever effected an immediate reduction in the general crime rate. He would have known that some crimes are easier to police than others, and that even the easier ones will only come down with meticulous and constant data analysis, and a scrupulous application of international best practice.

He would have cast his eye down the list of surging crimes and asked which are the most policeable and which the scariest. He would have chosen the ones that are both very scary and policeable, hijackings and retail robberies, perhaps, and called a press conference, a big one, one that sported the face of his minister, and perhaps even the deputy president.

At the press conference, he would have shared his stats with us. These particular crimes are surging, he would have said, and my job is to inform you about it and to do something about it. Here's what I'm going to do. I will call another press conference this time next month, the month after, and the month after that, and we will watch together, all of us, to see what is happening to these crimes. If what we are doing is not working, we will try something else.

It would not have worked magic. It would not have suddenly issued in the rebirth of South Africa as a safe country; we would not have begun to walk the streets at midnight with impunity. But we would have felt those responsible for public safety feeling our pain, empathising with our fear. We would have been left with the sense that the right people are losing sleep, working around the clock, working with professionalism and determination. We would have felt both hopeful and comforted.

Why can't the South African Police Service do this? The answer goes well beyond the police force, well beyond its commissioner and its minister. I think that the former liberation movement that is now our government is disenchanted, sometimes even shamed, by the nation it has inherited. The source of its inactivity is depression.

During the apartheid years, the liberation movement fashioned an image of the South African masses as inherently dignified, rising above their circumstances to throw off the shackles of oppression. Sure, there were pathologies, but nothing that couldn't be fixed by civilised public policy, nothing that couldn't be mended by the acquisition of power. If the cream of South Africa's activists and exiles had been canvassed on these matters in April 1994, I doubt whether any would have questioned the proposition that crime would slowly decrease, our overflowing jails begin to empty, our people find a good deal more peace and equanimity in the texture of everyday life.

Instead, governance has been hard, hard, hard; South Africa's pathologies so frustratingly stubborn. I think that under President Thabo Mbeki our government has begun to feel that the nation it inherited is dispiritingly and congenitally ordinary. Under Mbeki, a government has fallen out of love with its people, perhaps even feels shunned and betrayed by them.

And so it becomes too difficult for leaders to call a press conference and declare that they share our pain because the pain itself inspires too much shame. They cannot tell us that they will do their best to bring this and

119

that crime down, because they have become convinced that their best isn't good enough. Nothing is.

I think that our government is in a moment of depression. I think it is denying its depression. It needs to snap out of it. It needs to govern.

Hard-to-police crime raises some searching questions for South Africa

29 January 2007

Granted: the police are doing a poor job. One would struggle to find a South African who disagrees with that proposition. It is part of our stock of common knowledge, as incontestable as the fact that this morning's *Business Day* costs R6.50 on the streets. I wouldn't dare to disagree.

But I would add an important caveat. Even if we were blessed with the finest police force on the planet, some crimes, because of their slippery nature and because of the inherent limitations of law enforcement, do not lend themselves that well to policing. And sometimes, when the world is particularly unkind to us, policing the crimes we fear most can do more harm than good.

I am thinking in particular of house robberies. They are escalating in number; a few years ago, they happened in Gauteng an average of less than ten a day, last year at an average of almost 200 a day. They are also escalating in nastiness. A few years ago, one was held up at gunpoint while one's home was looted. In the last year, more and more house robbery victims have been held hostage; they are instructed to increase their daily ATM withdrawal limit, are forced to drive to the nearest ATM: the stuff of nightmares.

What can the cops do about this crime?

There isn't a quick answer. You can see why if you compare house robberies to crimes that are easier to police. Take car hijacking, for instance. Once a car is hijacked, its parts are distributed into a network, or it crosses international borders and enters a transcontinental bazaar. In other words, it enters an illicit market chain that police action can penetrate and weaken.

Not so with house robberies. Stolen cash doesn't enter a market chain. And the black market for electronic goods and household appliances is diffuse, highly dispersed, and thus much harder to police.

Take another example: street robberies. The majority occur on pedestrian causeways at twilight, dawn, or after dark in poorly lit spaces. A surge in street robberies is tackled by a combination of better lighting, targeted neighbourhood watch activity and visible policing.

Not so with suburban house robberies. They are often randomly dispersed across space and time. They happen in sprawling neighbourhoods, on deserted streets and behind high walls. To borrow a famous phrase from American criminology, sending out a patrol to look for house robberies is about as useful as sending out a fire engine to look for fires.

Good police managers tackle house robberies in two ways. First, crime analysts map house robberies in the hope of discovering that they do in fact cluster in some places and not others. The next task is to look for environmental factors that account for the cluster: proximity to a thoroughfare; trees covering streetlights; valley basins, rather than hilltops. But there is no particular reason why house robberies should cluster: when they do, and when something in the environment can be changed to stop them, the cops are lucky.

Second, those caught for house robbery are thoroughly debriefed in the hope that they are players in a fairly tight network. If the cops are lucky, those who rob houses in a particular police precinct all sell their stolen goods to the same people in the same neighbourhood. But again, there is no particular reason why this should be so.

What do cops do if they are not lucky? They revert to a far cruder form of policing; they drive around neighbourhoods searching for people on the street who look like they might be on their way to or from robbing a house. They stop and search them. If they find a weapon, and it's illegal, bingo. It is easy work, so others join in: neighbourhood watches, private security companies – soon, a whole lot of people in uniform are searching young men.

Does it work? A little. A house robber who knows that precinct A conducts pervasive stops-and-searches may choose to spend more time in precinct B.

The problem though, is the ratio of hits to misses. A recent British study found that in the UK one in 87 searches prevents or solves a serious crime.

What does that mean for the other 86? It means, essentially, that to be young, black and walking the pavements of a good neighbourhood is to stand a certain chance of humiliation; at some point a stranger's grubby pair of hands will rifle through your bags and pat your testicles.

That is something that was suffered with fear and bitterness under apartheid. Here and now, it escalates resentment, triggers displaced violence, and deepens mutual hostility.

The cops prevent some house robberies but tear our social fabric in the process. Is it worth it? I wouldn't like to be the one balancing the scales.

A lesson for South Africa's leaders in the art of the possible

16 January 2007

Some two years ago, sitting in the back of a police van in the early hours of a Sunday morning, I witnessed an ugly and unsettling incident that has stuck with me ever since. Its meaning has changed for me over time; of late, I have come to think of it as metaphor for governance in South Africa, as an astonishingly vivid representation of the cusp between national failure and success.

The place was a Gauteng township. I was doing field research, travelling with a police patrol. It was the Saturday night shift, 6.00 pm to 6.00 am, one of the busiest and hairiest times of the week for cops.

A couple of hours into the shift, I noticed that the two officers I was with were studiously avoiding one of their primary tasks. They were meant to be making themselves visible in 'hotspots', the blocks in which weekend street muggings and stabbings are concentrated. The prime hot-spot was the area around a large shebeen. The cops gave it as wide a berth as they could. They found red herrings to chase at the opposite end of their beat. When they had to move from one end of the township to the other, they traced an arc around it, going far out of their way.

I soon discovered why. At about midnight, they received a complaint that required them to walk into the dreaded shebeen itself. The complainant was a father whose son had driven his bakkie to the shebeen without his consent. The two officers dutifully reported to the shebeen, out of which some 300 or 400 people had spilled, some standing and drinking, others dancing. The officers identified both the bakkie and its young driver, and informed him that they would be escorting him to his father's house. He quietly agreed. As the bakkie was pulling off, six young men jumped onto the back, and it drove down the street, our patrol car just behind.

A few hundred metres later, the bakkie turned into a vacant field and stopped. The six men jumped off the back, and stood leaning against the bakkie, waiting for the two patrol officers to get out of their car. The moment they did so, the six men formed a tight circle around them and closed in menacingly. One of the six pointed at one of the cops and shouted his name. Then he called out the names of the cop's children, then the name of their primary school. He told the cop he was going to kill his family.

From that point on, the encounter became tightly choreographed. The cops were outnumbered three to one. They didn't stand a chance trying to arrest anyone. They backed away towards their car and radioed for help.

The thugs knew they had only three or four minutes left and made the most of their shrinking time, volleying gorier and more vivid death threats. The moment they heard the approaching sirens they bolted, each in a different direction. The two cops pursued them, but they were middle-aged and potbellied, the thugs young and lean, and from the back of the patrol car I watched them lumbering around like clowns.

I was impressed by the youngsters' performance. This was not a spontaneous outburst of drunken exuberance. Their display was thoughtful and tactically acute. In essence, the cops were being punished for straying onto gang turf. 'If you mind your own business,' the youngsters were saying, 'you'll be fine. But if you dare to police us, you will be hurt.'

A few days earlier, I had met the station commissioner, boss of the two cops on the Saturday night patrol. He was an affable man. Charmingly, he spent much of the afternoon I was with him quoting verbatim passages from Friedrich Nietzsche.

Now, in the wake of the Saturday night incident, I wrote him a memo describing what had happened.

His reply was defensive and a little pompous. 'Man has intimidated man for as long as history has been recorded,' he wrote. 'You are either wilfully ignorant or unbelievably naive.'

Welcome to my neighbourhood, he was saying. It's rough.

It was indeed a rough neighbourhood – I had seen that for myself. But he had just revealed himself as a particularly bad police leader, one who had forgotten that management is the art of the possible. Whether a bunch of teenagers scare cops into ducking their work is not a question of universal law, but of local leadership. His urgent task was to rewrite the rules the youngsters had so artfully laid down. They needed to know they had crossed a line. Intimidating cops into skirting a hotspot ought never to be cost-free.

I barely know the gregarious, Nietzsche-quoting station commissioner, and have no insight into the reasons for his beliefs. Perhaps it is that he is white, the township black, but I doubt it. Maybe it is that he is a fifth-tier leader in a massive bureaucracy and has reached the end of his career path long before retirement age. That's probably closer to the truth.

In any event, like millions of South Africans, he has internalised the idea that this is a country in which youths scare cops off the streets. The difference is that he is not entertaining his beliefs at home in front of the 7.00 pm news, but behind the desk of a police station commissioner. His beliefs thus become self-fulfilling. The world outside his window begins to resemble the one in his head.

This is but one example of many. I am talking too about the school principal who believes his is a country where it is impossible for a sizeable number of matriculants to pass higher grade maths; a district health manager who believes she lives in a place where people die of preventable disease within walking distance of a clinic as a matter of fact.

I am not punting the gobbledegook of the worst motivational speakers; I am not saying one need only will something for it to come true. There are enormous structural constraints. The health manager runs a district in which half the nursing posts are vacant, the station commissioner a precinct with too few vehicles, the principal a school without decent maths teachers.

Yet to call these deficiencies 'structural' is perhaps to pull the wool over one's eyes, for they are also symptoms of listless management: a decision to rationalise nursing colleges in the face of a great epidemic, a police leadership that has scurrilously underinvested in infrastructure for far too long.

In the last couple of years, travelling through South Africa's police stations, clinics and hospitals, I have seen too many institutional leaders slumped deadweight in deep resignation. They look around them and point wearily to the facts of the situation, not seeing that these 'facts' are the accumulated sediment of bad decisions; they are things that can be undone.

I wish for the state bureaucracy to borrow the inspiration of the six thugs I met that night two years ago. They were lean and clever, and they were fine practitioners of the art of the possible.

Centralised structure of police force no longer serves South Africa's needs

23 October 2006

How many readers of this column know that until three weeks ago the official in charge of policing Johannesburg was a man called Oswald Reddy? Or that he has a graduate degree in public policy from Harvard? Or that his job was dissolved earlier this month?

I'm picking on Reddy arbitrarily. I could choose Durban, or Port Elizabeth, or Cape Town. I'd hazard a guess that one in ten readers knows who heads the police in any of these places.

Why don't we know? Primarily because the cops in charge of policing South African cities are not accountable to us. They answer to their provincial commissioners, who, in turn, answer to a man with a big office in Pretoria called Jackie Selebi. And he, just of late, speaks to us as little as he can possibly help.

In short, we don't know the names of those who police the places we live because they are third-tier bureaucrats in a centrally managed monster of an organisation, one that fiercely believes its business to be none of ours.

Does this matter? It certainly does. I have lost count of the number of businesspeople who swear that all policing in Johannesburg needs is the recruitment of some talent and charisma from the outside. Something like a Maria Ramos in uniform.

Yet what would poor Ramos do if she became Johannesburg's top cop?

She would not be free to hire and fire, to attract talent by setting her own salary levels and conditions of employment, or to determine how much to spend on servicing old cars and how much on recruiting new constables.

Nor could we hold her accountable were hijacking to surge by 30% on her watch. She would have to refer us to Selebi. And he doesn't talk much.

Why are we stuck with this national monster? After all, best practice from most of the world tells us that good police forces are city police forces, that managing citizens' safety from a single building in the administrative capital is a really bad idea.

Part of the reason is historical. In 1994, the African National Congress (ANC) government inherited a hotchpotch of disreputable and incompetent homeland police forces. It had to close them down and absorb their personnel immediately. The only way to do that was to integrate them into the national police organisation the ANC inherited.

Moreover, back then the ANC was less concerned with crime fighting than with the stability of the police as an institution. The police force was an unknown. Would it become a springboard for a coup? Would its hundreds of bits and pieces all go their own way and do their own thing? It needed to be run from the centre.

But 12 years have passed since then and stability is no

longer the issue. Crime reduction is. I find it truly extraordinary that for all we talk about crime – and we do
indeed torment the life out of ourselves talking about it all
the time – the question of police accountability isn't on
the agenda.

I am not saying that decentralisation and accountability are the final word on crime. They bring problems of
their own, such as high-profile police managers more
interested in managing public perceptions than crime
itself. Neither crime nor the poor management of crime
fighting would vanish overnight.

But a great of deal of the pain South Africa is suffering
amid this latest crime wave is caused not just by crime
itself but by officialdom's mute, stubborn, and denialist
response to it.

Some months ago, Gauteng Safety and Liaison MEC
Firoz Cachalia allegedly pledged to resign if he failed to
deal with crime. The entire province instantly fell in love
with him. People were hungry for an official or a politician prepared to hold himself answerable to us.

The problem, of course, is that the police in Gauteng
are not accountable to Cachalia; they're accountable to
the man with the big office in Pretoria.

A few weeks ago, the South African Police Service put
into motion the most significant project of organisational
restructuring in 12 years. An entire tier of the organisation
is being dissolved, including the positions of area managers
like Reddy who run policing in our cities and towns.

Those driving the changes claim they are strengthen-
ing the grassroots, giving neighbourhood station commissioners the resources to manage their jurisdictions. Yet

insiders say the restructuring process is being managed haphazardly, and the organisation is demoralised.

This should be headline news. Selebi should be accounting for his plans at weekly press conferences. Independent experts on change management should be going into the organisation and telling us what they see. Yet we know next to nothing.

Reddy, by the way, is now the station commissioner at Honeydew.

The quiet eloquence of a good plan

14 August 2006

I know this isn't a fashionable thing to say at the moment, but Safety and Security Minister Charles Nqakula and police commissioner Jackie Selebi have been comporting themselves in recent weeks with a degree of wisdom and sobriety seldom attributed to them. I am thinking in particular of the long chain of events that followed the gun battle between police and a group of bandits in Jeppestown, Johannesburg in late June, which left four cops and eight armed robbers dead.

It was the sort of incident that, nine times out of ten, causes police leaders to produce terrible policy. By 'terrible' I mean policy that neither reduces crime nor makes anyone feel safer.

Consider the context: It was the last of a string of highly publicised incidents in which quasi-military groups of criminals wielding automatic weapons took over public spaces. Symbolically, such crimes are the worst of all; they convey the impression that the state has lost its monopoly over organised violence, that the world really is spinning out of control. In such circumstances, police leaders are under immense pressure to unleash a response that is seen and understood to be massive, uncompromising and retributive. In the process, effective policy gets turfed out the window.

In the hours following the bloodbath, it appeared that the police response was to be among the nine out of ten. Nqakula's first reported comment was hardly promising. 'Anyone who points a firearm at police,' he declared, 'will be killed by police officers.'

It was a puzzling thing to say in the wake of a massive gun battle. It was either a description of what had just happened, and was thus both empty and impotent, or it was a euphemistic announcement that guns were going to blaze and corpses mount.

And in the following days and weeks, the police did indeed begin to huff and puff, firing off their canons at nobody in particular, but they seemed to be doing so with only half a heart. For something had happened in the interim. The minister and the police chief went home to think, and think they did. Instead of the usual frenzy of aimless activity, they came up with something far more elegant. In early August, Nqakula walked out of a cabinet lekgotla and announced that the police had a list of 250 people who have made careers out of quasi-military crime such as bank robberies, mall robberies and cash heists. Specially constituted detective teams had been established in each province to find and arrest them.

Why is this a good plan? First and foremost, for what it isn't. The tired and lazy response would have been to assemble large numbers of troops, throw down wide cordons and take neighbourhoods by storm, waving automatic weapons in citizens' faces and searching every underwear drawer. Hardly a crackdown on those who rob banks and shopping malls, but something to put on the 7.00 pm news at any rate.

Nor were any of the usual red herrings planted: no talk of rewriting the legislation on the use of lethal force, no demands for stiffer sentences.

It is a good plan because it is sober and focused: it does neither more nor less than isolate the problem. Quasi-military-style armed robbery is a specialised activity. It is done by a finite group of qualified people. Whether 250 or 500 is anyone's guess. Nqakula may have sucked the figure out of his thumb. But it doesn't matter. Hunting every hijacker in the country would be stupid because everyone and their cousin can hijack a car. Hunting the limited networks behind quasi-military group-robbery is right.

Secondly, it's a good thing to do because it's doable. It sets the detective service and police intelligence a finite, graspable goal, one entirely within their remit and training.

And thirdly, setting concrete, achievable goals is good for morale and thus good for the organisation. Telling detectives to bring down robbery by 10% is demoralising; it is such an amorphous and impractical instruction that no-one knows where to begin. Telling them to find and arrest a couple of hundred people is ambitious but entirely tangible, labour intensive but gratifying.

At a more abstract level, the minister and the police chief have demonstrated an unusual degree of wisdom about what police services can and can't do. In the wake of shocking crimes, generation after generation of police chiefs across the planet have marched into press conferences and threatened to reinvent the wheel, knowing full well that every word was bullshit.

Nqakula and Selebi are doing the opposite. 'Okay,' they appear to be saying, 'There are many things we can't do. Here is something useful we can do.'

The cost of parliament's lazy 1997 sentencing decision

31 July 2006

When parliament passed legislation in 1997 mandating stringent minimum sentences for a long list of crimes, I was not the only one who thought the measure worse than useless. One needed only think about it a minute or two to see that if the aim of the new law was to reduce crime it was destined to fail.

In 1997, a person who hijacked a car in South Africa stood a 1-in-50 chance of being convicted for his crime. What might cause him to reconsider what he does for a living? Increasing his chances of getting caught and convicted to, say, one in four, would be sure to make him think again. But increasing his sentence from 10 to 15 years would surely not, since his chances of serving any time at all still remain a paltry 1 in 50.

Parliament made an old error, one that has been repeated countless times throughout history. Frustrated by their incapacity to increase the certainty of punishment, legislators increase its severity, deluding themselves that the substitution will do the trick.

I have always been sure that the legislation failed, but didn't have the empirical evidence to prove it. That changed earlier this year with the publication of a paper by Institute for Security Studies associate Antony Altbeker.

Minimum sentencing legislation came into effect in mid-1998. At much the same time, something extraordinary happened to South Africa's car theft and hijacking trends. In the two preceding years, absolute numbers of car thefts and hijackings rose by 12%. In 1998/99, the trend abruptly stopped and reversed. During the following six years, both crimes dropped by more than 21%.

This neat coincidence may suggest that the new minimum sentences were immediately and massively effective, that young men left the hijacking business en masse in fear of the 15 years they would now serve if caught. But before jumping to that conclusion you would have to ask yourself what they chose to do for a living instead.

The answer is not a happy one. During the very period in which car theft and hijacking were dropping, the rate of aggravated robbery, another crime onto which a minimum sentence of 15 years had been slapped, was rising sharply. Between 1996/7 and 2003/4, aggravated robberies consistently rose by more than 10% a year.

Altbeker does not argue that the surge in robbery is accounted for entirely by those who gave up stealing and hijacking cars. Nationally, he suggests, at least 15% of increased robbery can be explained by decreased car theft. But that is high enough. It tells us that a significant number of those who stopped stealing and hijacking cars began robbing instead.

What caused them to change occupations? Plainly and simply, it was the introduction of tracking technology in 1999. Suddenly, hijacking a car became like playing Russian roulette. The chances of catastrophe were never as high as one in six, as they are when one spins a revolver's cylinder. But for those who take cars every day or every week, encountering a tracker became a matter of time. Those with an appetite for high risk remained in the hijacking business. Those of more cautious bent bolted.

That so many of the cautious ones chose armed robbery as an alternative tells us with exquisite lucidity that parliament was barking up the wrong tree. A whole raft of South Africa's population of violent criminals began shifting occupation in response to changes in the odds of getting caught. And yet their calculations utterly ignored the recently promulgated changes in the severity of the punishment they might receive. If the question of jail time had entered their calculations, they would have left hijacking for unemployment, petty theft, or a place in the expanded public works programme – not for armed robbery.

Why does this matter? you may ask. Surely locking up hijackers and armed robbers for longer periods is good in and of itself?

It matters because the externalities are extremely severe. Countries across the globe that have introduced mandatory minimum sentences have soon lost control over their capacity to manage the size of their prison populations. In South Africa, chronic prison overcrowding had already reached alarming proportions by 1997. With the new sentencing law, the options in managing the problem narrowed to a few unpalatable alternatives. We can spend billions on prison-building; we can empty the jails of everyone except the most violent criminals; we can watch prisons overflow until they become so violent and disease-ridden that it becomes impossible for anyone to live or work in them.

The truth is that we are already doing all these things. Parliament made a lazy and careless mistake in 1997; the costs of its error mount every day.

A foot-long bush knife, a red-hot stick and a few words to the wise

8 May 2006

Three months ago, in a tiny village on the Pondoland coastline, I witnessed an encounter between a community and the police seemingly so wholesome and healthy I wondered whether I hadn't drifted onto the set of a clunky commercial advertising South African patriotism.

It was a Sunday morning. I was travelling in a patrol car with a solitary officer from a small-town police station. A radio dispatch sent us to attend to a complaint at an outlying village some 30 kilometres from the town centre. The complaint was of armed robbery and aggravated assault.

We arrived to find the entire community assembled and waiting for us – a gathering of some 600 people. The meeting was meticulously choreographed. Elderly and middle-aged men sat on benches and stools on the right side of the gathering. Married women sat on mats on the left. Young adults filled the space in between, most of them standing, some crouching on their haunches. Children wandered to and from a nearby tank carrying containers of drinking water.

When we arrived, two young women and a young man were pushed to the front of the gathering. The women described how, in the middle of the night, a man wearing a balaclava and holding a foot-long bush knife had climbed through their respective windows, woken them, and demanded their cellphones. Both had resisted and had been stabbed in the side of the head. Each lifted her hair to show the gathering her wounds.

'While he was climbing back out the window,' one of the young women narrated, 'I grabbed a hot stick from the stove and stabbed him in the back of his left shoulder. I heard his flesh singe.'

Both girls roused their parents, and at dawn the following morning a group of village elders spread out and went from door to door, demanding that each young man remove his shirt and show them his back. Within half an hour they had found a teenaged boy with a fresh bruise on his left shoulder. The police were called and the village assembled and waited.

After the young women had spoken, the suspect was pushed forward and told to talk. He mumbled inaudibly for a few minutes; the gathering waited patiently for him to finish. When he was done, the officer put him and several elders in the back of the van and drove to his home. The small group assembled in his bedroom, and the policeman began turning out his bed, his trunk, and his drawers. He was very poor, his room almost bare. The wall behind his bed sported several pictures of naked women torn out of magazines. His mother stood in the doorframe watching, her hand in front of her mouth. Between his mattress and his bed boards, the policeman found a foot-long bush knife.

We all climbed back into the van and returned to the

gathering. The bush knife was displayed to the assembled village, which murmured appropriately, and the policeman sat down on a chair, produced a pile of forms, and began taking statements. It was a drawn-out affair. Four statements in all – the two girls, an elder, and the suspect's father. Each took at least 30 minutes. The officer pulled his chair very close to his witness, and each testified in quiet tones.

Throughout this procedure – a period of about two hours in all – no-one moved and no-one spoke. All six hundred pairs of eyes watched every stroke of the police officer's pen. Occasionally, some restless youngsters would begin to stroll and chat. The moment they obstructed the line of vision between the policeman and the elderly men on their benches, they were shooed away; the old men wanted to see: they did not want to miss a single moment.

When the last statement was signed, the policeman stood and the gathering quickly dispersed. By the time we were back in the van, people had begun going about their business.

Driving back into town, the suspect locked in the rear of the van, I asked the policeman whether he had coached the two young women at any point during their testimony.

'Just once,' he said. 'I told them not to mention the balaclava. I told them to say that the man was barefaced, and that they recognised him.'

'And they listened to you?' I asked.

'Yes.'

'Why did you do that?'

'Just to be sure,' he said. 'The community had gone to such trouble: if that boy gets off, they will never lay a complaint again.'

Scorpions' birth was poisoned

30 March 2005

This article was written while the Kampepe Commission was hearing evidence on the future of the Scorpions, in the wake of the pasting the organisation received for the manner in which it went after Jacob Zuma. Prominent figures from across government and the ruling party were calling for the Scorpions to be absorbed into the police.

What are the implications if the Scorpions are absorbed into the South African Police Service, as is looking increasingly likely?

Some time in 1998, about a year before the Scorpions was formed, I did a background interview with one of the grand old men of European policing. He had recently reached the end of a long stint as the head of one of Europe's largest police agencies and was visiting post-apartheid South Africa for the first time. I asked him for his impressions.

'The South African government is doing a fine job,' he said. 'But there is an alarming gap: you do not have a top-notch enforcement capacity to protect the upper echelons of the state from organised crime and corruption. A

145

clean state is your most valuable asset. It is the question upon which your success as a country ultimately hinges. You can't expend enough effort or spend enough money protecting it. You will probably have to take resources away from street policing to do it, but you need to create an FBI-like agency.'

At the time I thought the retiring police chief's take on South Africa a little dodgy. Four years into democracy is not a good time to be taking resources away from street policing. New citizens need to be looked after. Feeling less safe ought not to be among one's first experiences of democracy.

Then Deputy President Thabo Mbeki, however, took this line of thinking very seriously. He didn't take money away from street policing but, in the months preceding the 1999 elections, he asked a cabinet subcommittee to draw up a blueprint for precisely the sort of agency the European police chief was urging upon us, and he let it be known there would be money to spend.

The blueprint that emerged was very impressive indeed. It bore the hallmarks of a smart, creative group of institution-designers, lifted by the prospect of managing a blue-sky project from conception to brick-and-mortar. The new agency would be placed in the justice department, not simply in order to be led by prosecutors, but because its designers wanted it to mark a clean break from the history of South African policing. Its staff would not consist of seconded police detectives, but of bright young graduates trained in global best practice, rather than in the residues of South Africa's pre-constitutional policing traditions.

The new agency's designers were acutely aware of the

looming problem of rivalry with the police. Indeed, they were obsessed with it. Early discussions were dominated by how to anticipate and diffuse turf wars. Marketing and branding experts were called in to give presentations to the cabinet subcommittee on how to build the status of the Scorpions while protecting that of the police. It was agreed that if the leaders of the two organisations closed ranks, their respective staff would follow.

Above all, the new agency's designers stressed that it would only succeed if it had strong political protection. Building a new enforcement tradition from scratch requires time and patience. The agency would need the space to find its feet. Some of its cases would threaten powerful interests. It would not fare well in a hostile environment.

In the end, very little of what was envisaged came to pass. Above all, the Scorpions did not get the political protection its designers sought. When it was conceived, it had a great deal of cabinet support, primarily in the form of Justice Minister Dullah Omar and Safety and Security Minister Sydney Mufamadi. By the time it was born, after the 1999 elections, the political environment had changed dramatically. The new safety and security minister, Steve Tshwete, once claimed he was so fond of the Scorpions he gave it its name. Yet insiders insist that he displayed hostility to the new agency from the start. His police commissioner, Jackie Selebi, was a sworn enemy.

Indeed, the new agency was left to be championed by its boss, Bulelani Ngcuka, who was not a cabinet minister, and needed to hunt for allies among his political principals.

The Scorpions thus had to prove itself too quickly, and as a result it made some grave mistakes. The handful of temporary secondments from the detective service, envisaged as a bridging mechanism, became a bucketful of permanent appointments. The result is that the agency began life poaching elite personnel from its rival. It also created the potential for a nasty fault-line within its own ranks: old white cops in senior positions, young black university graduates in junior ranks. Indeed, levels of morale inside the organisation have never matched its sharp, energetic brand.

The careful management of anticipated inter-agency rivalry envisaged during the Scorpions' conception never materialised. The new agency was born on the back foot in an extremely hostile environment. From the start, it tried too hard to win friends and to burn enemies.

Less than six years after its formation, the Scorpions is on its knees. The issue that has brought it there is precisely the one that so animated the old European police chief in 1998: the protection of the upper echelons of the state from organised crime and corruption. The arms deal and the parliamentary travel scam have been its unmaking.

The Scorpions' enemies claim that it has been hijacked by the interests of surreptitious political forces in the ruling party's succession battle. Its defenders retort that it is being destroyed because it is trying to do its job.

Both sides are missing the point, which is that the variables around its formation were so poorly handled that it was born to fail. In regard to matters of high-level corruption it was never going to be in a position just to do its job; it was never politically secure enough to handle matters so hot.

If the Scorpions is absorbed into the police, the meaning of the event will be quite clear and simple: we have tried to build an agency designed to protect the upper echelons of the state from organised crime and corruption, and we have failed. We just don't have the kind of state that can create such an agency.

It may be comforting to point out that we are hardly alone, that older and more established democracies have fared little better. The US during the Clinton presidency was not a pretty sight: a relentless war of attrition in which politicians grabbed every legal instrument at their disposal to humiliate and destroy their enemies. And as for the Italians under Silvio Berlusconi – we have nothing on them. In the early 2000s, Berlusconi appointed the lawyers who ran his legal defence in his corruption trials to the Justice Commission of the Italian parliament. They would fly to Milan in the morning to defend their client in court, and then to Rome in the afternoon where they would write the legislation designed to absolve him.

So, we have hardly hit rock bottom, but that is cold comfort. The point is that we embarked on a pretty consequential project of institution-building in 1999, and we were not up to the task.

Feeling dirty

29 November 2004

I have seldom met a middle-ranking South African cop who has not told me that his or her work is undervalued. On the one hand, this is predictable and boring. What human being wedged somewhere in the middle of a 130 000-strong bureaucracy does not feel ill-treated or hard done by? And yet, with cops there is something else going on when they tell you their work isn't understood, something as intriguing as it is disturbing.

First and foremost, their work is indeed misunderstood, not least by themselves. They are told, and many believe, that their job is primarily to arrest criminals and reduce crime. But this is, at best, what they do for perhaps 2% of their working lives. For the rest, their job is to clean up the mess human beings make when they fail in their lives and their relationships.

From domestic violence, to trouble between neighbours, to a pub brawl, to groups of kids harassing passersby, a cop's work begins whenever people cannot manage their relations with one another. A cop's job is, for the most part, to arrive at the scene of a crisis, one which the protagonists themselves cannot solve, and to make sure that things have settled down by the time he leaves. If he needs to arrest someone in order to settle things down, he will. But the arrest is instrumental, rather than an end in itself; it is a tool he uses to solve crises.

This is indeed a harrowing job, not least because it is unteachable. In the words of sociologist Egon Bittner: 'While lawyers, physicians, teachers, social workers, and clergymen also deal with critical problems, they have bodies of technical knowledge or elaborate schemes of norms to guide them in their respective tasks. But in police work there exists little more than an inchoate lore, and most of what a policeman needs to know to do his work he has to learn on his own. Thus, what ultimately gets done depends primarily on the individual officer's perspicacity, judiciousness and initiative.'

So, it is by its nature an undervalued job; nobody teaches you how to do it and, more often than not, nobody rewards you when you learn, by your wits, to do it well. It is something you succeed or fail at alone, or with one partner, on the streets.

But there is a far more profound and unsettling reason why cops feel their work is undervalued. There is a great deal of darkness in human beings and a great deal of unhappiness in human relationships. A cop is called to the scene whenever this darkness erupts into something ugly, something unmanageable. His job is to find a provisional solution, on the hoof, to this eruption of the ugly and the upsetting.

A cop's work, in other words, is to deal with the dirt human lives spew, and some of this dirt sticks to him. I am not sure how to express this thought except by way of

151

example. A couple of years ago, I was with a cop who was called to the scene of a complaint at a private home. She was not told what the complaint was about. It was 2 am. We arrived to find a woman sitting on a deck chair in the garden, staring vacantly, drunk out of her mind, a half-empty bottle of beer in her hand, several empty beer bottles at her feet. Inside the house, two kids, both under the age of three, lay sleeping.

The cop stared at this woman, contemplated the thought of two toddlers, late at night, uncared for by a sober adult, and lost her temper. She slapped the beer bottle out of the drunken woman's hand and dragged her by the scruff of the neck into the back of the police van.

This wasn't good policing. It was an eruption of emotion, the sort of emotion a cop is meant to contain. But the cop was also a working mother, one who spends nights away from her children in order to provide for them, and she found herself staring a failed mother in the face. The personal and the professional mingled and became indistinguishable. In that split second when she lost her temper, she became a cop-mother, and there was no separating the two.

That is a cop's work – the professional is personal; the work hurts. Their vocation is to mire themselves in the debris of human failings. It is not only undervalued. It isn't acknowledged at all.

A quiet leap forward in South Africa's policing

1 November 2004

Profound changes seldom wear their meaning on their sleeves. They slip innocuously into the rhythms of daily life. You have to look to see that they are there.

I spent last Wednesday morning accompanying a routine police patrol in Kagiso. Wednesday mornings are quiet. Nothing out of the ordinary happened. And yet, everything that happened was out of the ordinary. Everything that happened had seldom happened before in the history of South African policing.

At 7.30 am, a call came over the radio that a group of boys was vandalising a public phone on Kagiso Avenue. The patrol van arrived on the scene two or three minutes later. In the event, there was no vandalism – just an ugly altercation. The youngsters were herded into the back of the van and driven to their primary school. The cops phoned their parents from the principal's office to tell them what their kids had been up to.

At 8.15 am, the patrol got a call from the principal at a high school. We were in his office six or seven minutes later. He said there was a sweets vendor operating from a caravan on the road behind the school whom he suspected was selling drugs to his students. The cops strolled across the school grounds, walked around the back of the caravan, and took the vendor by surprise. They searched him, the roof of his caravan and the depths of his sweets packets, and found no drugs. They got him to sign an undertaking to move his caravan into his yard, several blocks away, within 48 hours.

Later in the morning, the patrol came across a teen-aged boy crossing the road with a large section of a prefab wall strung across his shoulders. They stopped him, asked where he had got the sheet, and made him accompany them to the site where he had found it.

The boy protested, said he had done nothing wrong. 'Wherever you got that sheet,' a patrol officer replied, 'there is a problem. If you stole it, I want to know from whom. If you took it from a vacant property, I want to know why it is vacant, who owns it, what they are doing about occupying it.'

Why is any of this important? First, because it is new. None of these innocuous stories could have been told in Kagiso three years ago. Back then, the entire township was policed by two patrol vans and a single response vehicle. No police officer had the time to phone truant boys' parents, or to bother to stop a boy carrying building material on his shoulders. Today, Kagiso is policed by five, 24-hour patrols, each assigned to a fixed sector of the township. Ten years into democracy, there are, for the first time, sufficient police numbers in the township to do ordinary policing.

And as for the more distant past, as for the apartheid era, policing in townships was never about managing the small disruptions to daily life. Blood had to spill to attract police attention. Emergency services were about carting the injured into ambulances, the dead into mortuary vans, and beating the living daylights out of suspects until they confessed.

So, it is new, but why does it matter? Anyone who has been on patrol will tell you that the bulk of a cop's time and energy is spent neither preventing crimes nor catching criminals, but responding to emerging crises of disorder, conflict, unhappiness – in other words, to micro-disruptions to daily life. As the sociologist Egon Bittner has put it, the role of a police officer is to respond to any situation, 'as long as it could be said that it involves something-that-ought-not-to-be-happenening-about-which-someone-had-better-do-something-now!'

This function is so rudimentary, and yet incalculably important. Any populated space which does not have recourse to a neutral authority whose task is to manage emerging crises is brittle, frayed, on edge. Sometimes this brittleness expresses itself in the sudden eruption of conflict. Sometimes it is expressed merely in a feeling of unease – an intangible, nervous sense that the world is unsafe simply because there is nobody watching.

Slowly, in places like Kagiso, this most basic police function is beginning to emerge. The benefits are as impossible to quantify as they are invaluable. Will it bring crime down? Perhaps not directly. But that is not the point. The well-being of a community cannot be measured in a simple count of recorded crimes. It is also to be measured in intangibles like peace of mind, security, and predictability.

Steinberg was in Kagiso for an Institute for Security Studies research project on sector policing on the West Rand.

What crime stats measure and what they don't

18 October 2004

For all the heat generated by South Africa's interminable debate about the accuracy of our crime statistics, one simple but crucial story seldom gets told. In nine cases of out ten, a policeman's job is not, strictly speaking, to solve a crime, but to diffuse a crisis. Whether he makes an arrest, and thus records a crime, usually depends on one thing only: whether he thinks it will help him manage the crisis. In other words, crime stats are less a reflection of how often people beat, stab and steal from each other, than of how different cops handle the same situations.

A few months ago, I interviewed two beat cops who had just come off a Friday night shift. That night, they had responded to five domestic violence complaints. In each case, they arrived at a disturbed and unhappy home inhabited by a drunken man and traumatised women and children.

How to deal with this situation? The first step in answering this question is to ask what, precisely, the character of the situation is. It is a crime scene, to be sure, inasmuch as somebody has been beaten or threatened. But for the cop who responds to the call, the fact that it is a crime scene is the least of his concerns. More pressing is that there is a problem, and that he has been called to manage it. What must he do for the 15 minutes he is in that home to ensure that his presence makes things better rather than worse?

The first thing he must assess is whether the perpetrator ought to spend the night in the house. To throw him into the back of a police van in front of his family is to humiliate him. And a humiliated man may well come home the next day and wreak vengeance on his family. So, the cop decides not to arrest: he mediates until the tension has subsided, and promises to come back in a few hours to see that everything is in order. He hopes to God this was the right thing to do: if somebody is stabbed or shot in that house later in the evening he will have a death on his conscience.

Alternatively, the cop may decide that the situation is too volatile for the violent man to remain in the house. He takes him in for 'questioning' – which is really just a means to get him out of the house – locks him in the police station cells for a few hours, and hopes that by the time he returns home he is sober and calm. Hopes, rather than knows. He will only be sure in retrospect whether his decision was right.

There is a third option: the cop urges the complainant to lay charges. She agrees, the violent man is arrested, the detective branch is called, a case is opened, and a domestic violence crime is recorded. Was this the right decision? The cop is not sure. He complains that he is not a social worker, that his policeman's tools are too blunt to deal adequately with family trauma.

The two Friday-shift cops I interviewed believed, from long experience, that arresting men for domestic violence makes matters worse, that it escalates conflict. So, in all five calls, they did not urge the complainant to lay charges. They recommended that she contact a local victim support centre and seek a protection order against her husband, and they took him in for 'questioning' to get him out of the house for the night.

The following evening, two new cops worked the same shift, but they had a very different philosophy. They also responded to five domestic violence calls, but in four cases, they urged the complainant to lay charges. They knew that the charges would probably be dropped on Monday morning, but they felt that the justice process, even if not followed to its conclusion, would act as a powerful deterrent.

So, according to the crime stats, there was no domestic violence on the Friday night, but four cases on the Saturday night. What had changed? Different cops, radically different stats. The Friday night cops weren't trying to keep the stats down; they were trying to do their jobs as best they knew how. So were the Saturday night cops.

With the exception of some crimes, like murder, hijacking and the theft of insured property, crime stats are less a reflection of crime levels than an opaque and not especially useful record of how different cops perform their work.

Temper vengeance with reason to break cycle of violent crime

26 July 2004

I wrote this column in response to a Business Day *editorial arguing that all violent crimes should carry a life sentence of hard labour. The editorial was written in the wake of the murder of Leigh Matthews by a fellow-student at Midrand College.*

The indescribable devastation etched on the faces of Leigh Matthews's parents when they received news of her death was enough to pain anyone who saw it. It was also enough to trigger feelings of vengeance against those who murdered her. This is not just understandable – it is appropriate. Those who cause unspeakable suffering must suffer in turn; that is part of what justice is about.

Justice has another task, though, and that is to reduce crime levels. Reducing crime and seeking retribution are not the same thing. While they both have a place, they shouldn't be conflated.

It was argued in these pages last Friday that punishments in South Africa are not horrible enough. The prospect of '20 years in prison watching television and three meals a day' is insufficient to deter violent criminals, it was argued. 'Any crime of violence ... should automatically attract a life sentence of toil, without parole or comfort.'

That can't be right. For one, if existing conditions in maximum-security prisons aren't enough to deter, nothing is. Spending 15 hours a day locked in a room with 40 people controlled by violent gangs is no holiday. Many inmates I have spoken to would rather live a life of toil; the idea of working with one's hands, getting fresh air, doing anything at all – even digging a hole in the ground – can become the stuff of fantasy.

If harsher prison conditions aren't enough to deter violent criminals, they certainly are enough to drive offenders back to crime.

When I visited a maximum-security prison in the Western Cape in February 2002, a young inmate caught my eye and asked if we could talk. I will call him Sizwe. He told a story which his mother later repeated to me. His mother is a domestic worker. She scrounged and saved and borrowed, eventually getting enough to enrol Sizwe at a Model C school. And so he was given an unlikely opportunity, but he threw it away. He felt socially foreign at school, had learning difficulties, was unhappy. On the eve of his grade 11 exams, which he knew he would fail, he hijacked a car together with two young men with whom he had grown up in Langa. He was caught and sentenced to 15 years in prison.

I met him a month after he had been sentenced. He was pretty desperate. He told me he wanted more than anything else to continue studying and get a matric. He wanted to do so first and foremost for his sanity, and secondly for his future. He couldn't study at a maximum-security prison; he would have to wait several years before being eligible for a transfer to medium security status.

A year later, I met Sizwe in the contact visiting room at his prison. His eyes were glazed, he mumbled incoherently and stared at the floor. He had nothing to say to me. I found out from a warder that he had joined the 26 prison gang, stabbing another inmate as part of his recruitment ritual. That is life in a maximum-security prison; such was his survival strategy.

I can guarantee you that when Sizwe comes out of prison, he will put a gun in somebody's face once again. He may use it. That is all he will be good for. And he will be very good for it. Members of the 26s are scattered across every town and village in the Western Cape. Through the networks he built in prison, he will have access to black markets in any contraband you can think of. He will not have access to any other opportunity; crime is what he will do for a living.

In saying these things, I am at one with the Correctional Services Department. One of the long-term goals in its latest white paper is to put offenders in a position to live normal lives after they are released. May they succeed.

You may consider this argument morally unacceptable. Why give a carjacker access to education and a tolerable life when he threw it all away by his own volition?

But what are the alternatives? Kill him? Keep him in jail until he dies a natural death? Aside from anything else, it isn't clear that these measures are sufficiently deterrent to justify themselves.

If we are not going to kill him, there is only one alternative: don't carve out a murderer's life for him. Vengeance is right, but when it isn't tempered by reason, it blows up in our faces.

Pretty white girl in chains

17 January 2003

I recently had occasion to read through a pile of newspaper reports and readers' letters, published in *Beeld*, on the Tanya Oosthuizen case.

For those who have forgotten, Oosthuizen is the most famous and beguiling criminal in the history of white Pretoria. In 1999, the year after she matriculated with three distinctions from the prestigious Pretoria High School for Girls, she and four teenaged white boys were arrested for a string of armed robberies conducted in the bourgeois suburbs of Pretoria. Most of their victims were of the same social milieu as the gang's parents: Afrikaans, middle-class and middle-aged.

Oosthuizen had spent the evenings of her matric year working as a prostitute at an upmarket escort agency. During that time, she met and fell in love with André Venter, a budding career criminal.

Venter was jailed during the course of their affair. Tanya wanted to raise money for his legal representation. And so, the newspaper stories go, she seduced four teenaged boys into committing several armed robberies with her to raise money for her lover's legal defence.

The *Beeld* reports and letters make for tantalising reading. The essence of Tanya's story was that things in the newspaper's heartland were disturbingly awry. Whites had begun to erect walls and electric fences around their suburbs, convinced that the pathologies of crime and violence were carried by blacks and came from outside. News of a band of armed robbers, born and bred in the Pretoria elite, rattled the white middle class.

The newspaper's readership was hungry for a story that would both name and quarantine the illness Tanya represented. *Beeld* duly obliged. Evidence that things were not right with Tanya from the very beginning began to emerge. Her father was a depressive who allowed the family business, a farm, to collapse. As a young teen, she had overheard her parents discussing the possibility of family suicide. A little later, she and her father developed a disturbing ritual. He, depressed, suicidal, would lie naked in his bath. Tanya would sit with him in the bathroom, trying to coax him back to life.

So the story quickly evolved into a morality tale, as tabloidy as the best of them. Building a Calvinist family in this day and age, the tale informed, is not easy: family businesses go bankrupt, the economic climate is uncertain. And the cost of failure is severe: allow your daughters to wander from the strict confines of a stable family and they will come back sexy and wicked, seducing your sons into crime.

It was as if the walls and electric fences of the new South Africa were not enough: the symbolic walls, which protect the young from perverse adventures, must be built even higher.

Most interesting, perhaps, was how scandalised readers

were when *Beeld* published a front-page photograph of Tanya entering court in leg chains. 'Is it necessary to humiliate her and her family like that?' one letter-writer asked. 'You are perverse and disgusting,' another reader railed at *Beeld*.

The anger sparked by the spectacle of Tanya in chains says so much about the confused and ugly expectations an embattled white community places on the criminal justice system. For implicit in the rage is the belief that we should really have two justice systems, each run on rival principles.

Chains and jails are for the dangerous classes; the justice system must warehouse those we fear until they age and become harmless. But a pretty white girl who strays – her soul is mendable, and the justice system must indeed mend it, preserving, all the while, the dignity that inheres in her class, her status, and the colour of her skin.

It is a pity *Beeld*'s heartland missed a wonderful and rare opportunity. The cultural proximity of the accused, the disturbing feeling that she could have been one's own daughter, drove home to *Beeld*'s readers the crazy tragedy of criminal justice, the wasting of a human life.

If the heartland had stretched its empathy a little further, beyond the barriers of race, it would have realised that Tanya's awful fate is the fate of all who are convicted of serious crimes. We warehouse those we fear, packing them in overcrowded cells until boredom and fatigue turn them into animals who stab and kill over a watch or a piece of meat.

Perhaps, if the newspaper's readers had thought about it just a little more, they would have wondered why on earth we haven't invented a better way of dealing with those we fear.

Off the beaten track in South African police maze

1 August 2002

Reading through a South African crime researcher's notes the other day, I came across a story so extravagant in its intrigue and its cynicism, it appeared to come straight out of a James Ellroy novel.

An internal investigations detective – a cop who snoops on other cops – was found shot dead in his car one morning in 1999 in central Johannesburg. Nothing was missing from his briefcase save a single docket, which diarised his investigation into a station-level intelligence officer, suspected of working for a gun merchant. Fingerprints taken from the scene matched those of a Zimbabwean immigrant named 'Collin'. Collin was a police informer, his handler none other than the intelligence officer suspected of gun running.

In splendid Ellroy-esque fashion, the story ends there. Collin flees the country and the evidence is too spindly to pin anything on his handler; business-as-usual resumes.

It wouldn't do to exaggerate; Johannesburg does not resemble a fully-fledged Ellroy-esque universe, where every senior police manager works for someone in the underworld and clean cops put their heads down and notice nothing.

For one, the structure of the Johannesburg under-world does not allow for that sort of corruption. There are no extensive crime hierarchies with the means to capture the public administration of an entire city; there are only thousands of entrepreneurs with lots of connections and a good head for new markets.

Nonetheless, the story of Collin and his handler does capture the texture of a worrying syndrome, one that says much about the strange journey our police force has travelled since the transition to democracy.

Any student of policing will tell you that a cop's career path is capricious and unpredictable. Promotion rests on the evaluation of one's performance, yet a cop's perform-ance is notoriously hard to evaluate. Much of his work happens where no police supervisor can watch. And be-sides, even within the confines of a single police station, what counts as good work is always up for grabs.

The result, as American policing theorist Carl Klockars has pointed out, is that every cop 'must be prepared to witness people move ahead of him or her who have no better qualification for doing so than a political connec-tion. This cop must do so without going sour ...'

If this is true of police forces universally, it was all the more so in South Africa in the mid-1990s. In the midst of a traumatic transition, one that was badly handled by police managers and politicians, the police force lost its anchors. In the minds of many cops, both black and white, the organisation had become utterly unpre-dictable; there were simply no markers to follow if you wanted to get ahead.

Against this backdrop, many cops substituted loyalty to

individual managers for loyalty to the institution. Backing a real-life dispenser of power seemed a better bet than relying on an unreadable organisation. Spend some time with a South African cop and you see these networks of loyalty in action. Everyone relies, both for morale and resources, on an informal circle.

In the vice neighbourhoods of inner-city Johannesburg, where prostitution and drug peddling is both pervasive and organised, circles of loyalty soon turn into circles of corruption. A crime boss puts a unit commander on his payroll and soon a deep pocket of local cops is on his side.

The problem becomes insidious when the unit commander gets promoted to area level, then provincial head office. Then the pocket of bad cops has stretched too far; the crime boss's money begins paying for policy and strategy.

How serious is the problem? It is hard to say. Many inner-city detectives tell stories of area office requisitioning and then losing their dockets. In the late 1990s, in the coloured townships of western Johannesburg, an expensive anti-gang violence project was incessantly sabotaged from on high.

As I said earlier, this is not James Ellroy's crazy world of 1930s Los Angeles. But it is worrying enough to take notice.

The good news is that the police force has settled considerably since the mid-1990s; it is a happier and more predictable place. The bad news is that a force as massive and unwieldy as ours will always, to some extent, appear to its members as a Kafkaesque bureaucracy. The problem might be structural, but structural reform will, on its own, never be enough.

The best remedy is the most difficult: the laborious, expensive and dangerous work of busting enough bad cops to make corruption itself too unpredictable a career-path to follow.

That is what the internal investigations detective was doing when Collin killed him.

Steve Tshwete did little
to raise police morale

17 May 2002

In the wake of Steve Tshwete's death, a few journalists and a well-known analyst said that the late minister's abiding achievement was to have lifted police morale.

In a country where most media bodies lack the resources to follow up every story, off-the-cuff comments from a handful of pundits often count for truth; soon everyone was saying Tshwete had lifted morale.

It is mean-spirited to assassinate the character of someone fresh in his grave, and I do not want to say that Mr Fix-It was a bad or a foolish man. Tshwete's virtues – he was a gifted orator, his appetite for the art of politics was extraordinary – are pretty obvious.

Yet, in my experience, Tshwete did little to lift police morale. Indeed, his association with South Africa's policing was as unremarkable as it was brief. I say this not to set the record straight for its own sake. The reasons his short stay at Wachthuis was unremarkable are less of a comment on the man himself than on the organisation he led, and telling the story illuminates a great deal about that arcane institution.

Tshwete's dramatic roadshow in the winter of 1999,

when he first took office, remains etched in the mind. He took his dark glasses and his sand-and-glue voice to township stadiums across the country, and he breathed fire. 'We will unleash the might of the state upon [criminals],' he told an audience of 1 500 police at Soweto's Jabulani Amphitheatre.

Speaking specifically to the black police members in the audience, he continued: 'Your offices in the townships are a disgrace. You cannot do your jobs from a toilet. We will build you decent offices.'

Walking out of the amphitheatre after the speech, I overheard a black policeman with sergeant's stripes on his shoulders mutter to a colleague: 'Just like Vlok. Just like Adriaan bloody Vlok.'

Intrigued by the eccentric comparison, I asked the man what he meant. 'Politicians come and go,' he said, 'but we'll be here long after they've moved on.'

The sergeant's comment was pregnant with everything that is strange and inscrutable about the world South African police inhabit. He was not comparing Tshwete to apartheid South Africa's most notorious police minister; he was simply comparing him to another outsider.

The police's institutional memory is long and deep; it has its own logic, one that sometimes transcends the most volcanic changes South Africa has experienced, even the transition to democracy.

Stand in front of Wachthuis – the wide, grey building in downtown Pretoria that houses the police command – and you begin to get an inkling of this logic. Wachthuis sits in the middle of town like a giant mole, its relationship with the rest of the organisation a bit dim-sighted.

Forty-two policing areas, 1 100 neighbourhood stations, innumerable specialised detective units, support units, logistical units: it is a monster of an organisation, each of its myriad parts a world unto itself, driven by the steam of its own eccentric legacy.

As far as organisational communication is concerned, it is as if Wachthuis is connected to the rest of the organisation by a vast system of underground pipes. The chief shouts down the blower, and by the time his message reaches its destination it is an odd, distorted echo.

What did Tshwete's voice sound like at the other end of the pipes? He said criminals would be walloped, that the police would wallop them both inside and outside the confines of the Constitution.

Foolish police took succour from their new minister's words. But good police? They knew that, whatever Tshwete said about the Constitution, it would still be there tomorrow. So would the judiciary, and the clever '*liegfabriek*' law firms that represent the rich criminals.

The truth is that the police were battling with the Constitution, and they needed somebody to say something intelligent about it. They needed someone to teach them how to spar with it, how to find its loopholes, test its limits. They were practitioners, after all, and they needed to understand the Constitution the way a tax lawyer understands tax law, the way an investment banker understands forex rules.

Long before Tshwete arrived at Wachthuis, the new crew – the African National Congress (ANC) minister and his new batch of officials – gave up trying to say anything useful about the Constitution.

They left legal matters to the police's legal services department, an institution run by a hyperbolically cautious bunch of old-timers. These police lawyers treated the Constitution with palpable fear, interpreting new laws with mind-boggling conservatism. They interpreted a draft lethal force law, for instance, to say that police could only shoot while being shot at. Now that did very little for police morale.

So, when Tshwete got to Wachthuis and started speaking about walloping people inside and outside the confines of the Constitution, bad police thought that heaven had arrived on earth. Good police sighed with resignation. They knew that their fresh minister meant well, but they also knew that practically, in their day-to-day work, his words meant nothing.

Soon Tshwete settled into Wachthuis and got on with his stuff, and the cops at the other end of the pipes got on with their stuff, and occasionally they thought about each other. Good police have learned, through their own intelligence, how to use the Constitution. Bad police lose cases every day, every hour, because they do not have a clue.

When Tshwete died, many police felt a little sad for the big-hearted, larger-than-life man at headquarters. But their sadness was for an outsider, whose presence in their lives and their organisation was always going to be fleeting.

Does this reflect badly on Tshwete? Perhaps, if you are feeling ungenerous. But it does reflect well on South Africa. The police is the largest armed force in the country. Not that long ago, the ANC worried about that. It bent over backwards to ensure that the guns would never point in the wrong direction. Today, the sudden and untimely death of a charismatic leader does not make that much difference. Things are stable, they go on, as they should.

ABROAD

Acceptance in Manhattan versus apprehension in Johannesburg

21 May 2007

Sometimes it takes a single moment in a foreign city to understand simple things about the place you inhabit back home.

I spent the last Saturday morning of April in Tompkins Square Park on the east side of Manhattan. Most of the people there were young and very well groomed. They stood around and chatted while their dogs sniffed one another in the park's leash-free enclosure.

I needed to find a men's room. I spotted one at the northern end of the park, walked through the door and found myself on another planet. The place was packed tight with black and Hispanic men, leaving little room to move. Some were at the urinal, others huddled in threes or fours, murmuring quietly. A row of toilets lined the far wall, the cubicle doors and walls long ago stripped and carted way. A man sat on each toilet with his trousers around his ankles, the sound of faeces hitting toilet bowl punctuating the gentle mumbling of men in conversation. It seemed from the way they inhabited this place that these people spent a lot of time here, that they were using it in well-established ways.

I went back outside and watched the white people and their dogs. It was immediately apparent, from the sounds, from the ambience, from that indescribable sense of mood and spirit public spaces exude, that the dog-runners were not only untroubled by the men in the toilet: they were oblivious to them.

A few days later, I met with an acquaintance who has lived close to the park for decades, and told her my tale. 'Good grief,' she said. 'I did not even know that there was a public toilet in the park. I in fact don't ever recall seeing a public toilet in New York.'

I find it an extraordinary story for what it says both about New York and Johannesburg. In the 1970s, Tompkins Square Park was the epicentre of the East Village's heroin epidemic, in the 1980s, its crack epidemic. At 1.00 am on an August morning in 1988, armed police stormed the park, ostensibly to enforce a curfew. The homeless resisted. What followed became known as the Tompkins Square Park Riot, a two-day-long urban battle.

That is now forgotten history. The Saturday morning I walked into the park, the American economy was entering its fifteenth year of growth, and the colonisation of Manhattan by the long boom's beneficiaries was well established. The middle class is now so thoroughly in command of the city, its rules of conduct so firmly stamped on public space, it barely notices that anyone else is there. The homeless meekly insinuate themselves into the cracks, their knowledge that the lion's share of space belongs to others now deep in their blood.

Compare this to the leafy places where Johannesburg's

middle classes hang out. A couple of years ago, a group of homeless people began gathering in the eastern corner of a small park across the road from my flat. Within weeks, a residents' association had formed to lobby local government to have them removed. The park is now surrounded by a tall green fence with a locked gate and stands empty.

Rich and poor cannot share public space so easily here. It is too dangerous. The rules of engagement are insufficiently clear. Why?

The answer is resentment. It is absent in the Manhattan park, but present in spades here. Watching the poor of Manhattan, I marvelled that there was not a trace of it. Whether they genuinely felt no anger at the inequality rubbed in their faces, or whether they had simply learned to repress it, I do not know. I'm not sufficiently familiar with New York to understand. Perhaps it is the consequence of a decade and a half of very tough policing. Perhaps it is the deeply ingrained American ideology that anyone can make it, and that the world is thus fundamentally fair.

In Johannesburg's public space, the poor bump up against the rich to ask rhetorical questions about why things are as they are. Sometimes the questions take form as a hostile glance, sometimes as sarcastically obsequious panhandling. Sometimes young men simply occupy space, their knowledge that their mere presence is dangerous a source of hollow satisfaction. The rich live in a permanently furtive state, always on the lookout for trouble.

As in New York, Johannesburg's bourgeoisie is reaping the benefits of a long boom. It is something of a triumph, expressed in a taste for flashy cars and gaudy homes. But unlike their American counterparts, Johannesburg's rich have not taken control of their city. On the contrary, they fear it like the plague. The reason is that the middle class's ascendance carries a stamp of legitimacy there, but not here.

Lessons in security from Bogotá

3 July 2006

'Every time I go to cabinet to make a presentation,' I remember a senior South African police manager telling me some time in 1998, 'I thank God for Bogotá. Take away the capital of Colombia, and you're explaining to the president why you preside over the most violent city on the planet.' Indeed, in the late 1990s, when I reported on policing for *Business Day*, Bogotá was less a place than a sigh of relief. It was famous in South African security circles as the blessed name near the top of the Interpol chart, always above Johannesburg, listing the murder capitals of the world.

So when I visited Bogotá last month I was thinking of crime. Not that I was given much choice. At the airport, a pre-recorded message blasted through the immigration booths in incessant relays: caution – only use official yellow cabs; demand to see the driver's nametag with photograph. In my hotel room, a bold-lettered notice posted on the back of the door advised guests not to go out alone, never to go out at night, to spread cash between several pockets, and not, under any circumstances, to give one's name and address to men in uniform. At the cellphone shop, the task of getting a local SIM-card took the better part of an afternoon: proof of identity, of permanent address, place of employment ... nobody gets a working phone unless security agencies can trace you.

Yet once the paraphernalia of arrival were complete and I stepped out into the city, I found myself half a world from home. In contrast to South Africa's metropolitan cities, apprehensiveness about crime in Bogotá, it seems, is something reserved for foreign visitors. The Johannes-burg bourgeoisie's fear of their city is signalled by their invisibility: the streets of middle-class suburbs are empty, their inhabitants at home or in the bowels of shopping malls. Bogotá's middle class inhabits its city in unselfcon-scious comfort.

In the late afternoon on a public holiday I found myself walking through the streets of a suburb of tall apartment blocks. The world was brimming over with people. A shared public space, about two kilometres long and a couple of street blocks wide, stretched across the suburb's eastern border. Sandwiched between the natural boundaries of a bus terminus to the north and a six-lane highway to the south, it consisted of a park, several sports fields, a string of walkways, cycle lanes, a cinema complex and an outdoor market. The entire space was bound together by a network of pedestrian bridges, wide enough to constitute public spaces themselves.

It seemed that the entire neighbourhood had descended on this two-kilometre stretch. There were elderly people on sticks and Zimmer frames, many solitary people read-ing books or newspapers in the sun, teenage lovers blind to the rest of the world, their tongues down one another's throats, an infinite relay of soccer games between children and their fathers.

In the livelier parts of town, like the trendy urban suburbs to the north of the city centre, the public areas are larger and fuller: blocks of space, several kilometres long and wide, dense with restaurants and clubs and shops, alive until well after midnight.

When I asked Bogotá residents what accounted for the ease with which they inhabited their city, they all had one answer: good public policy. Everyone mentioned that the murder rate had dropped about 70% since the mid-1990s. They spoke of a former mayor, Enrique Peñalosa, whose tenure in the late 1990s and early 2000s changed the city. Peñalosa's renewal programme, they said, was essentially about creating public space. He attacked private-vehicle use with a string of prohibitive measures, and coupled this with the introduction of a ubiquitous bus system. He built several hundred kilometres of bicycle pathways, created or renovated more than a thousand parks, built countless plazas and pedestrian walkways. The two-kilometre strip of communal neighbourhood space I walked through must have been one of his creations.

Yet there were two things I noticed immediately which Bogotá residents didn't mention, perhaps because living in a city blinds one to its peculiarities. Walking through that neighbourhood strip, or indeed, through any other of Bogotá's crowded spaces, I never once looked up without seeing a man in a uniform carrying a gun. Whether it was soldiers in their fatigues carrying assault rifles, or police, or private security guards, public space was saturated with firearms. In Bogotá alone there are a staggering 160 000 private security guards, a larger number than the entire staff of the South African Police Service. When I was a child a schoolteacher told me there were so many spiders in the world that one was always watching me. In Bogotá, it is armed men who always watch you. They are everywhere.

And indeed, whenever one leaves these guarded public spaces, this city of 7.5 million feels pretty rough. The people I met were all middle-class professionals who lived in the north of the city. Most had never set foot in the poor southern neighbourhoods, not once in their lives. I didn't get to these parts; my hosts wouldn't have known the way. They did know that there are zones one must move through very quickly. Driving along a thoroughfare just south of the city, the panhandlers at the traffic lights tried to pick the car locks. The young men offering to clean the windscreen were clearly thinking of smashing it.

Another thing I noticed immediately, which a citizen of Johannesburg cannot fail to see, is that Bogotá's middle classes live primarily in high-density neighbourhoods. They inhabit public space because that is where they live their lives – they have no choice. Reclaiming public space is thus the obvious public-policy option, and not particularly difficult. Build the two-kilometre strip of communal land, and people are sure to claim it as theirs. In a high-density neighbourhood with a park, a cinema, a market and a posse of armed men, it is possible to live much of your life without fearing crime.

And that is the primary difference between Bogotá and South Africa's major cities. Our middle classes have never lived urban lives. In one of his essays, JM Coetzee describes the mid-1950s South African suburbs of his youth as among 'the ex-British colonies ... rapidly becoming cultural provinces of the United States'. He is exactly right: those are the two influences that gave South African suburban life its character.

The colonial influence, made possible by cheap land and labour, shaped spaces and lives that barely touched this continent; lives lived in social clubs, sports clubs and in large residential gardens. Then came the American inspiration: long, broad highways, the celebration of the family car, the construction of sprawling suburbs.

Common to these influences is their anti-urbanism. They fashion lives lived behind walls, around swimming pools and family tables. Public space is largely empty. Johannesburg mayor Amos Masondo may fancy taking inspiration from Bogotá's Enrique Peñalosa, but he is unfortunate enough to have inherited the wrong sort of city.

The Johannesburg middle class's proper response to its Bogotá counterpart ought perhaps to be one of envy. There it is possible to inhabit a fortified zone so wide one can imagine it goes on forever.

A moral also in our unheroic responses to catastrophe

25 July 2005

Saturday fortnight, 6 August, is the sixtieth anniversary of the day the Americans dropped an atomic bomb on Hiroshima. There will be solemn ceremonies and worthy speeches, and they will be broadcast across the world. Many Japanese leaders and intellectuals will tell us, as they did on previous anniversaries of the dropping of the bomb, that Japan is special; that it alone has witnessed, as victim, humanity's capacity to destroy itself; that Japanese memory of that day is still humanity's most powerful weapon against self-obliteration.

These are worthy and useful things for the Japanese to believe about themselves and to tell us. For we stand a slightly better chance of preserving ourselves as a species if we talk ourselves up to the task. But there are other worthy and useful lessons to learn from Hiroshima – one of them is how flesh-and-blood people actually behaved towards one another in the wake of the bomb.

Few survivors recall acts of solidarity between strangers in the immediate aftermath of the nuclear explosion. In John Hersey's book, *Hiroshima*, an extraordinary work of reportage on the experiences of six people who survived

186

the bomb, the author records the recollections of a survivor, Kiyoshi Tanimoto, of the first hour after the blast: '... Mr Tanimoto saw, as he approached the centre [of Hiroshima], that all the houses had been crushed and many were afire. The trees were bare and their trunks were charred ... Under many houses, people screamed for help, but no one helped; in general, survivors that day assisted only their relatives and immediate neighbours, for they could not comprehend or tolerate a wider circle of misery.'

As much as our need to believe in redemption urges us to couple stories of mass suffering with stories of heroism, there are few heroic tales from the morning of 6 August 1945 to tell. In the face of indescribable devastation our worlds contract, rather than expand. On that day, the city's survivors suffered collectively but alone.

Even years later, after the dead had been mourned and Hiroshima rebuilt, the event remained as much an occasion for estrangement as solidarity. In describing those who lived through the bombings, the Japanese steered clear of the word 'survivor', for fear that a celebration of survival would insult those who had died. Instead, survivors were given the agonisingly neutral designation, *hibakusha* – 'explosion-affected persons'.

In some respects, the Japanese government was reluctant to recognise the presence of *hibakusha* at all. It took until 1957, for instance, for the Japanese Diet to pass a law giving material assistance to survivors, many of whom were left permanently disabled or chronically ill.

In the marketplace, too, survivors found themselves the victims of silent ostracism. 'Non-*hibakusha* employers,' Hersey writes, 'developed a prejudice against the survivors

187

as word got around that they were prone to all sorts of ailments, and that even those ... who were not cruelly maimed and had not developed any serious overt symptoms were unreliable workers, since most of them seemed to suffer ... from the mysterious but real malaise that came to be known as one kind of lasting A-bomb sickness: a nagging weakness and weariness, dizziness now and then, digestive troubles, all aggravated by a sense of oppression, a sense of doom, for it was said that unspeakable diseases might at any time plant nasty flowers on the bodies of their victims, and even in those of their descendants.'

Ironically, then, at a time when commemoration of the bomb had taken its place as the centrepiece of Japanese identity, those who had suffered directly were facing the consequences in isolation, for society at large felt decidedly ambivalent toward them.

I am not at all attempting to rubbish the noble and powerful things that are going to be said on 6 August. Nor is my intention to insult Japanese memory. What I am saying is that the legacy of catastrophic events, especially those caused by human aggression rather than nature, is always Janus-faced. When we think of these events in the abstract, we are capable of forging powerful bonds of solidarity. The British welfare state was built in the wake of the wartime bombings. And Japan's quest to become the richest nation on earth took much of its inspiration from the memory of wartime suffering.

But when reminded of the actual concrete and flesh of catastrophe, we are far less generous. Everyone lives in fear of death. And those who carry the mark of death about them are difficult to live with, difficult to embrace and accept.

Planning to avert the unimaginable

18 April 2005

At 10.14 am on 11 September 2001, US Vice-President Dick Cheney instructed the North American Aerospace Defense Command to order its fighter pilots, who had been scrambled over America's northeastern seaboard some time earlier, to shoot down any aircraft, including passenger jets, that failed to respond to radio communication. In hindsight, the instruction didn't matter since all four hijacked planes had crashed by then. But the White House did not know that at the time; it knew that the World Trade Centre and Pentagon had been hit, and it reasoned that there might be other hijacked planes in American skies, heading for targets.

Eighteen months later, the US Congress's 9/11 Commission interviewed the commander of the Northeast Air Defense Sector, whose task it was to relay the vice-president's order to the fighter pilots circling New York and Washington. He told the commissioners he did not relay the order because he was 'unsure how the pilots would, or should, proceed with this guidance'. And so, the commissioners noted in their report, 'while leaders in Washington believed that the fighters above them had been instructed to "take out" hostile aircraft, the only orders actually conveyed to the pilots were to "ID type and tail"'.

It is an extraordinary story about the limits of institutions. The North American Aerospace Defense Command had been established during the Cold War to defend the US from airborne attack. Hardwired into its cognitive structure was the notion that any attack to which it might have to respond would come from the ocean in the form of a missile. The idea that its task would be to shoot down a passenger liner was unimaginable. And so an order delivered on behalf of its supreme commander was in essence ignored on the grounds that those tasked with executing it would not know how to respond.

The story gets more interesting. For to say that Cheney's order was unimaginable is not true. Such an order had been imagined three years earlier. In 1998, Bill Clinton's counterterrorism chief Dick Clarke chaired an exercise which, according to the 9/11 Commission report, 'involved a scenario in which a group of terrorists commandeered a Learjet ... and flew it towards a target in Washington, DC.' During the exercise, 'officials from the Pentagon said they could scramble aircraft ... but they would need to go to the President for rules of engagement, and there was no mechanism to do so. There was no clear resolution of the problem at the exercise.'

Imagination was not the problem: it was the gap between imagining and experiencing. US security agencies had to experience a devastating terrorist attack in order to begin preparing to prevent one.

And that is what they have been doing ever since – a

gargantuan, sprawling, machine has spent more than three years getting its many heads and limbs around the task of stopping a repeat of 9/11. Car traffic flows around airports have been redesigned to make detection of reconnoitring vehicles easier. Airport staff have been trained to detect telltale behaviour patterns in people carrying bombs. In every major US city, F16 jets are on standby to shoot down an airliner within minutes of being alerted.

As for threats emanating from the sea, US officials are now stationed at every harbour on the planet with a direct line to an American port; their task is to profile each US-bound cargo container for dirty bombs. Countries like South Africa have been exhorted to spend billions upgrading harbour security.

Yet for all this, there is little doubt that an elegantly planned conspiracy will break through these new defences. To take just one example: more than 24 000 containers are offloaded at US ports every day. Searching each one would bring trade to the US to a standstill. Instead, about 3% is searched. A great deal of thought and money has gone into ensuring that the right 3% is fingered, but certainty is impossible. The US cannot prevent another attack short of sealing its borders and teaching its citizenry subsistence farming.

Indeed, the re-engineering of America's defence machine is motivated as much by concerns about political legitimacy as about security. The US administration knows there may well be an attack it is unable to prevent. It also knows it must be able to say it did all it could, that it went to the brink of the possible.

So, America's fighter pilots are now prepared to shoot down passenger liners, but it is George Bush's legacy, more than anything else, that is made more secure as a result.

Football and melancholy: the quiet of a defeated city

4 July 2004

I was in Buenos Aires the day Argentina crashed prematurely out of the 2002 FIFA World Cup. The match against Sweden, which Argentina had to win to stay in the tournament, was scheduled to start at 3.30 am.

At around midnight, our host (I was with three other foreign journalists) began to get jittery.

'No-one knows what will happen if Argentina don't win,' he said. 'What with the economic crisis, who knows? People may loot shops, overturn cars ...'

He was anxious about us foreigners wandering the streets in the aftermath of an Argentine defeat. 'If you must go out,' he said, 'wrap yourselves up in Argentine colours, don't speak to anyone, and go straight home.'

Argentine nationalism is the strangest hybrid of emotions, both wonderful and sad. Everybody is from somewhere else. Welsh-Argentine, Yugoslav-Argentine, Italian-Argentine – even some who have been here three or four generations carry in their heads the invented memories, and often the languages, of a home to which they have never been.

It is wonderful because Argentina welcomes anyone

and everyone; its nonchalant comfort about difference is awesome.

It is sad because its national pride is palpably brittle. Bad times bring in their wake the hollow and inarticulate drama of feeling inferior, a wistfulness about being somewhere else.

I met an 81-year-old women who spoke to me in perfect English, her accent more Eton than any self-respecting Etonian would tolerate. 'I'm tired of Buenos Aires,' she told me. 'It doesn't compete with the great cities of the world. It has nothing to offer.'

'What is your favourite city?' I asked her. 'Paris, London, Rome?'

'I don't know,' she replied. 'The furthest north I've ever been is Mexico City, and that is a very uncivilised place.'

The city's identity is written all over its architecture. Each of the trendy inner-city suburbs to the north of downtown is a stylised slither of western Europe. Pieces of Chelsea, Charlottenberg, the Marais, all jumbled together in the space of a few square kilometres.

Last December, when the peso was delinked from the dollar and lost 60% of its value in one afternoon, Buenos Aireans were rudely reminded that they live at the bottom of a troubled continent. By the end of January, vast swathes of the Argentine middle class had been catapulted into indigence. More than 50% of the city's homeowners had defaulted on their monthly mortgage payments. Credit had been bought in US dollars, and besides, a blanket freeze on personal bank accounts meant that even those whose savings had not evaporated could not access them.

Driving into downtown, it is palpable that you are entering a city in shock. The gigantic advertising boards on the side of the highway and on top of the skyscrapers are all blank. Down in the streets, the cavernous, southern-European-style cafés that punctuate each block are brightly lit and entirely empty. The elderly Buenos Airean waiters inside, with their immaculate white jackets, their black bow ties and lugubrious faces, stare out into the street.

At 3.30 am, when the match against Sweden began, the downtown cafés were full, every one of them, for the first time in a long time. On the streets outside, the only vehicles to pass were municipal buses, on schedule, every 15 minutes, each one empty.

The entire city had decided that this was a spectacle to be experienced together, in public.

Nobody spoke during the game. The only sounds were the sucking of gums and the rapping of nervous fingers on tabletops.

When Sweden scored against the run of play, even these ticks and rattles vanished. A woman at the far end of the café took off her clothes and watched the remainder of the game in her underwear, giant tears rolling down her cheeks. Nobody batted an eyelid.

As the final whistle blew, the cafés emptied. Two minutes after the end of the game, and it was just the old waiters again, pacing their forlorn and vacant tables. Outside, the streets were suddenly gridlocked, as thousands upon thousands of people made their way home. The pavements were crammed with pedestrians, all wrapped in the Argentine blue and white, heads lowered and silent.

It was a truly extraordinary spectacle, dreamlike and

eerie; an entire city on the streets and not a single word exchanged.

Since the December crash, Buenos Aires has been an unsettled, bad-tempered place, prone to sporadic street violence and bar room brawls.

But on the day their team was beaten, something special and quite gentle happened. A whole city mourned together in silence, unified in their depression, as everyone displaced their months of private anguish onto 11 defeated football players and their crestfallen coach.

War-ravaged Middle East sorely needs civilised leadership

5 April 2004

When the Israeli right wing runs out of sentences and phrases to describe its take on the world, its last resort is two simple words: 'suicide bomber'. What easier way to demonstrate that it is engaged in a clash of civilisations; that its enemy is utterly irredeemable?

The transformation of a human being into a bomb could scarcely be undertaken, the argument goes, by people immersed in a secular, humanist culture. We are dealing here with something atavistic and unfathomable; these are not people like us, not people who understand reason and negotiation.

It is instructive to remember that this is a rehearsal of a familiar argument, that we have been here before. Sixty years ago, the US's leaders were telling America that the West was embroiled in a clash of civilisations. Back then, the foe was 'The Yellow Peril', the Japanese, and the primary evidence of their decrepitude and madness was the kamikaze pilot, the lunatic who, like today's suicide bomber, sacrificed his life in order to kill.

Sixty years is long enough to erase memories; we forget

197

how viscerally Americans hated the Japanese. Writing in his private diary in July 1945, US President Harry Truman called the Japanese 'savages, ruthless, merciless and fanatic'. Less than a month later, days after he ordered the nuclear destruction of Hiroshima and Nagasaki, Truman wrote in a personal letter that 'when you have to deal with a beast, you have to treat him as a beast'.

Truman's feelings were not eccentric. Ernie Pyle, America's most celebrated war correspondent at the time, filed a report from the Pacific in mid-1945 describing his first sighting of Japanese prisoners of war. 'They gave me the creeps,' he wrote, 'and I wanted a mental bath after looking at them.'

Also in 1945, Frank Capra, the celebrated Hollywood director, made a film for the US Army in which the Japanese were described as 'photographic prints off the same negative', a line that came to emblematise American contempt for the Japanese.

'Prints off the same negative' is of a piece with the image of the kamikaze pilot; he is not a human being, but a mass-produced industrial artefact.

In hindsight, of course, this writing off of a civilisation as subhuman is laughable. By 1952, just seven years after Truman's 'beast' letter, Japan was the US's staunchest ally in the Pacific; it was governed by the most progressive constitution ever written; and it was about to become the most prosperous nation on the planet.

And as the lid was lifted on Japanese archives from the 1930s and 40s, so the world came to understand something about the place of the kamikaze pilot in wartime Japan. Far from being 'prints off the same negative', the Japanese of the early 1940s were in a state of very human turmoil. Among the more interesting things scholars found in Japanese government intelligence reports of the time was the word *kyodatsu*, meaning exhaustion and despair. Japanese intelligence officials used it to explain why, when Emperor Hirohito visited air-raid shelters in Tokyo, ordinary residents greeted him with listless disrespect. They also used it to account for the ubiquitous presence of antigovernment graffiti across Tokyo in 1945.

Nobody ever conducted a poll among Japanese at the time on what they thought about kamikaze pilots. Given what has been learned about that time though, it is probable that a great many understood them as a grotesque symptom of the nihilism of war.

I am not about to argue that Palestine is a replica of wartime Japan. That would be patently ridiculous. I am making one simple point. In the heat of conflict, when people are dying terrible deaths, sweeping aspersions cast on entire races and civilisations – aspersions that are revealed as ludicrous in the sober light of peace – gain powerful currency. Ever since the commencement of the second intifada, the idea that Palestinians are the products of a civilisational disaster has been a potent undercurrent in Israeli politics. It is this undercurrent that has carried Ariel Sharon down a disastrous path.

Last November, a poll conducted among Palestinians in Gaza and the West Bank found that 55% favoured a negotiated settlement based on 1967 borders and a return of Palestinian refugees, not to their original homes, but to a new Palestinian state. Three polls conducted over the last two years found that a slim majority of Israelis want the same.

The problem in the Middle East is not a clash of civilisations, but an absence of civilised leadership.

MacArthur mystique absent in Iraq

8 December 2003

Sitting in his barricaded Baghdad fortress, does Paul Bremer, the US's chief bureaucrat in Iraq, ever think of General Douglas MacArthur? Such daydreaming must be sheer torture.

MacArthur governed occupied Japan between 1945 and 1951 with an arrogance unthinkable in today's Iraq. He saw his task as a God-ordained mission to bring American virtues to the ignorant; he likened the maturity of Japanese civilisation to that of a twelve-year-old boy; said he was going to force-feed democracy down Japanese throats morsel by morsel.

By any reasonable account, he was gloriously success-ful. He left Japan with one of the most advanced constitu-tions on the planet, a constitution which, 50 years later, remains healthy and thriving.

Poor Bremer – oh, to be born at the wrong time.

If you think I'm exaggerating about MacArthur, con-sider only his censorship policies. Under his tutelage, Japanese educators paged through history textbooks and blocked out references to Japanese imperialism with black ink. Pictures of Japanese battleships also had to be erased.

Samurai movies were banned, lest they instil feelings of warrior pride. Scenes of Mount Fuji – a symbol of Japanese nationalism – were cut from films.

Part of Japan's problem, MacArthur believed, was that it was just too damned inhibited. So he decreed that there should be kissing in Japanese films. He banned books and films about the bombing of Hiroshima. He even banned John Steinbeck's *The Grapes of Wrath* for its vivid depiction of American poverty. And lest anyone notice that he was fostering freedom of expression by dictating how Japanese express themselves, he banned any mention of occupation censorship.

As MacArthur himself pointed out, the terms of the occupation gave him absolute power: 'I not only had the normal executive authorities … I had legislative authority. I could by fiat issue directives.'

And he played the part with wonderful imperiousness. During his six years in Japan, the general seldom left his office. His private secretary claimed after the occupation that MacArthur met with only 16 Japanese more than once, 'and none of these was under the rank, say … of Chief Justice.'

Middle-ranking American officers commandeered upper-class houses from their Japanese owners and employed cook 'boys', maids, nannies and laundry 'girls' to take care of their families – all paid for by the bankrupt Japanese government. Indeed, at a time when its cities were flattened and much of its citizenry indigent, Japan was forced to bankroll every cent of the occupation.

Yet, American personnel were never once attacked. When MacArthur left in 1951, Tokyo's school kids were given the day off and the road to the airport was lined with thousands of well-wishers. Tokyo's leading daily, *Asahi*, lauded him: 'As if pleased with his own children growing up, he took pleasure in the Japanese people … walking step by step towards democracy.'

Why, Paul Bremer might despair, did this neocolonial maniac meet with such success? One reason is that, by the end of 1945, ordinary Japanese had painfully awoken to the fact that they had been the victims of a colossal folly. More than three million countrymen and women had died because an ultranationalist regime fed ethnic triumphalism and racist vitriol down the nation's throat for more than a generation. After the war, there was a craving in Japan for foreign ideas. By 1948, several dozen Marxist, existentialist and feminist journals were in circulation; some commanded readerships of hundreds of thousands. When Jean-Paul Sartre's novel, *Nausée*, was released in Japan in 1946, it shot to the top of the bestseller list and stayed there for a year. Japan was truly hungry for the West.

Thinking of MacArthur, Paul Bremer may well be wondering whether the bright sparks in Washington haven't made an epic mistake. Did they confuse today's Middle East with yesterday's Japan? Did they think that under the dross of Saddam's fascism and the ayatollah's fundamentalism, the people of the Middle East were truly hungry for the West?

It was an article of metaphysical faith, a dogma. The growing hatred of America in the Middle East couldn't possibly cut that deep. Everyone living under a dictator yearns for freedom, and everyone who yearns for freedom must surely love America.

Bremer was to be a tempered, civilianised MacArthur. The Arab masses were to be the Tokyo citizens queuing for Sartre.

Among all its other meanings, the occupation of Iraq is a devastating moment of American disenchantment. 1945 is gone. The Star-Spangled Banner will never again mean the things it once did. And it hurts like hell.

Ailing Japanese postwar social pact far from ready for burial

10 November 2003

It is old hat among anthropologists that if you want to understand a city you ought to observe how it buries its dead.

Among the most valuable pieces of real estate in downtown Tokyo are the vacant spaces in its cemeteries. They are auctioned off at staggering prices, and the chief buyers are not families or individuals but private corporations.

Senior executives in Japanese firms are buried, not by loved ones, but by 'The Company'. At the funeral, the colleagues of the dead man sit in hierarchical order and are the first to pay their respects; his family sits in the second row. The proceedings are managed by the departed one's office staff, who direct mourners to their proper places and oversee the minutiae of protocol.

In this context, where the company looms so large it has eclipsed the family in matters of burial and death, you begin to grasp the existential fears that accompany the prospect of downsizing and labour market liberalisation. As Japan suffers its twelfth year of almost uninterrupted recession, you begin to understand why it has been so reluctant to embark on serious economic reform.

This strange, overbearing role the company plays – as benefactor, lifelong patron and burier – is not, as is sometimes claimed, a modern embodiment of ancient Japanese custom. It is the product of the ghastly aftermath of World War II, which saw Japan's major cities levelled and a third of its population rendered indigent. In the 1950s, the country entered into a pact with itself – one peculiar to nations that have suffered ubiquitous devastation – to educate, house and employ everyone. The private sector became more than a profit engine; it became a dispenser of largesse and welfare. It played this role with enthusiasm, knowing that if it did not, a militant trade union movement and popular socialist party were waiting in the wings to lead post-war Japan.

Forty years later, the fruits of this pact are still visible, not only in the funerals of senior company men, but in the jobs performed by blue-collar contract workers. A baffling array of superfluous functions has been invented simply to keep people employed. When a delivery van stops somewhere in the dense maze of narrow lanes that fill inner-city Tokyo, a veritable army of men equipped with luminous batons jumps out to redirect traffic; at the supermarket parking lot, a similar army awaits to guide you into your parking space; at the highway tollgates, the ticket-dispensing machines are automated, but they are staffed anyway.

Most of these costs are borne by the private sector. And the results are truly stupefying. In an economy that has been contracting for more than a decade, the unemployment rate stands at 5%.

Everyone in Japan knows that the pact has long stopped paying for itself. But the country soldiers on anyhow, as if in collective denial. Earlier this year, the government baled out one of the country's largest financial institutions, Resona, buying a ¥1.7 trillion stake in the bank, and it is still in the red. A few months later, the reserve bank took the extraordinary measure of ploughing more than a trillion yen into the stock exchange in order to maintain stock prices and thus defend the value of the financial sector's investments.

The country keeps telling itself that things must change. Every new prime minister since the mid-1990s has promised to clean up the financial sector and introduce a host of neoliberal reforms. None has. Countless CEOs have spoken of stripping the seniority system and replacing it with a meritocracy. It hasn't happened.

Instead, Japan sews patch after patch onto its frayed post-war pact, and for the moment, it can still afford to; decades of staggering growth have created massive reserves of wealth.

Yet the post-war political economy must die at some point. The question is how, and what will emerge in its wake. Some say the future will be ugly.

'Listen to Shintaro Ishihara [the popular governor of Tokyo],' a Japanese executive told me. 'He says Japan fought a just war in the 1930s and 40s. He says it is time for Japan to retrieve its old glory, to become the boss of Asia again. People love him.

'That may well be the voice of the future. When Japan is really wounded – when professionals are retrenched en masse and when the people who direct traffic are sitting on the pavement with begging bowls – the old nationalism may come back, and with it, a backlash against nearly 50 years of liberalism.'

Burden too much for clueless US

15 September 2003

It is often said of young people that they are not yet sure of the nature of the world around them, nor of how to negotiate a path through it. It is less often that such things are said of young empires.

Yet this is precisely what the British political theorist John Gray has written of the US in his recently published book, *Al Qaeda and What It Means to Be Modern*, which he penned on the eve of the coalition's invasion of Iraq.

'On the one hand,' Gray writes, 'Americans believe that all human beings are Americans under the skin. On the other hand, they have long viewed the world … as corrupt, possibly beyond redemption.

'This ambiguity in American perceptions,' Gray continues, 'is mirrored in [post-September 11] military policy. From one angle, it is an attempt to secure the US from attack. From another, it is one more effort to remake the world in an American image.'

You could see this ambiguity at work within the Bush administration in the weeks and months before the Iraqi invasion. On the one hand, the administration touted the notion that America's new foes are irrational, perhaps to the point of being suicidal, that their capacity for destruction must thus be squashed pre-emptively.

This is an expression of the second leg of Gray's ambiguity; the idea that zones of the planet are beyond redemption, that they are best dealt with by the exercise of America's unmatchable military power.

And yet, in the weeks leading up to the invasion, a very different understanding of the coming war emerged from the White House and the Pentagon, one which had very little to do with the doctrine of pre-emptive attack. The idea was that the spectacle of Saddam Hussein's defeat on satellite television would, like the fall of the Berlin Wall did in the Eastern Bloc, stir the Middle East's silent democratic majority to speak.

Hussein's downfall would inspire popular rebellion against Iranian clergy; Palestinian terror organisations would find themselves in a political wilderness, paving the way to a permanent settlement with Israel; even the Saudi polity would feel the murmur of an incipient democratic will.

This is the first leg of Gray's ambiguity; the idea that, muffled beneath the weight of tyrants, the people of the Middle East are equality-loving Americans.

From whichever pole of the ambiguity you look at it, Gray argues, the policies American strategic thought has spawned will make a poor job of maintaining an empire.

The idea that the US's mortal foes can be quashed by pre-emptive attack on sovereign states is wrong-headed, especially when the most potent of those foes is not a state but a terror network. The Bush administration has so often rammed down our throats the notion that terrorists need the connivance of states to survive, we have forgotten that this has never been true. Sectarian terror in Northern Ireland, for instance, flourished for decades in British territory.

As Gray argues, the war on terror has as much chance of success as the war on drugs. Both terror and the drug trade are hybrid networks of global exchange, not armies; neither is vulnerable to frontal attack.

Military policy premised on the conviction that people are American under the skin is even more dangerous. We are living in an age where the world's relation to American culture is volatile, unstable and ambivalent, where ideas and artefacts are simultaneously loved and hated precisely because they are American. US occupiers cannot also be liberators – the world's relation to America is too painful, too complicated.

As the US's grasp on post-war Iraq slips, much of the world looks on with barely concealed glee, delighted that the superpower is getting its comeuppance. Yet the celebration is hollow. There is, in fact, no cause for comfort.

If the tasks of empire do indeed drain America of its resources and its will, the rest of the world will suffer along with it. If the world's largest producer and consumer is badly injured by its ventures abroad, the era of global trade that has just begun will surely end, battering economies like ours horribly.

Politically, it is possible that a global community of nations would fill the vacuum left by the superpower, containing regional conflicts by the application of a common

set of rules. More likely though, is an epoch of precarious-
ness and instability.

Gray's argument, that the young American empire has-
n't a clue how to deal with its burden, is the nastiest I've
heard in a long time.

Bill Clinton's undoing was not to have lived in interesting times

23 June 2003

Bill Clinton has a favourite joke. He told it several times during his embattled presidency:

'A guy is walking along the edge of the Grand Canyon and he falls off. He's hurtling down hundreds of feet to certain death and he looks up and grabs this twig, and it breaks his fall. He heaves a sigh of relief, and then, all of a sudden, he sees the roots coming loose. He looks up to the sky and says, "God, why me? I'm a good person. I've taken care of my family. I've paid all my taxes, I've worked all my life. Why me?" And this thunderous voice says, "Son, there's just something about you that I don't like."'

You can understand Clinton's bashful self-pity. He believes he was one of those rare presidents, the sort who comes around once in a generation, who has the finesse and the imagination to change a nation's understanding of itself. He believes that he could have been great, a political genius, if only he had had the chance.

He didn't; he had the misfortune to govern America during the only eight-year period in modern history when there was nothing great to do. Just behind him lay the drama of the Cold War, just ahead, the catastrophe of 11 September

2001. The last decade of the twentieth century was an unlikely interlude, in which America had no enemies and hubristic intellectuals with short memories declared that history itself had ended.

Interludes are bad times for politicians. With nothing epochal at stake, politics is reduced to a series of vicious skirmishes, as nasty and unbecoming as they are parochial. In Clinton's era, the stage was dominated by small-minded men, the Newt Gingriches and Kenneth Starrs of the world. They brought all the muckiness of civil law into politics and they used it to destroy and humiliate, to rake and to revel in dirt.

Clinton, a man riddled with foibles and weakness, was their cannon-fodder. He will not be remembered for cleaning up the mess of Reaganomics and balancing the budget, nor for tramping on stale, liberal shibboleths with an imaginative welfare-to-work programme, nor indeed for presiding over an epoch of economic prosperity. He will be remembered for Monica Lewinsky.

How would he have fared if fate had handed him another presidency in a more grandiose time? How, for instance, would he have done post-September 11?

In retrospect, with the presidency of George W Bush as a barometer, it is tempting to imagine that Clinton would at very least have made a tolerable post-September 11 president, and that the world we live in today would have been a far saner one.

For a start, Clinton would never have been seduced by the icy, apocalyptic vision of the planet that has animated the Bush administration's foreign policy. For all their talk about building liberal democracies in the Middle East, it

213

is clear, in the wake of the Iraqi war, that this is never what the Bushies had in mind.

Their vision is essentially of a planet divided into zones of progress on the one hand, and zones of culturally-determined darkness and hopelessness on the other. Their understanding is that the dark zones ought to be patrolled by the perpetual threat of overwhelming military might, that the borders of the dark zones ought only to be crossed to extinguish threats and to gather precious minerals.

For all the agonised indecisiveness Clinton may well have displayed post-September 11, he would have had the savvy to know that this horrible vision is self-fulfilling. He would have known that, if wielded imprudently, a superpower's might does indeed create zones of anarchic, inchoate resentment across the globe.

To be sure, Clinton would almost certainly have taken America's war machine into Afghanistan. But he would have taken care not to unpick the fabric of the institutions of global governance that were so carefully put together in the second half of the twentieth century. However problematically, he would have projected an image of American power mediated by the need for consensus and the imperative to play by global rules.

He would have been vilified for treading softly at a moment of crisis and for turning a blind eye to the unsavoury in the name of pragmatism. But one suspects he would have understood what it means to run a global empire during an epoch of instability. It is hard to imagine that he would have succumbed to the hubris and amnesia that characterises America's rulers today.

When New Yorkers sound like backwater Pennsylvanians

12 May 2003

In June 1999, a little more than two years before the September 11 attacks, South African-born writer and television producer Sandy Balfour attended a US armed forces airshow somewhere in backwater Pennsylvania. Eighty thousand people were there.

'The announcer at the air show tells us about the F-15 bomber, which, at that moment, is going through its paces in the sky above us,' Balfour writes in his memoir, *Pretty Girl in Crimson Rose.*

'It is, he goes on, a very fine aircraft. It has all you could ask of an aircraft – speed, power, range and versatility. What the F-15 is, (the announcer) concludes, "is a shining example of America's ability to kill anyone, anytime, anywhere, under any circumstances."

'The remarks drew from the crowd a great shout of appreciation and ringing applause, which chimed neatly with the roar of the F-15's engines as the pilot pointed its nose to the heavens and disappeared into the sun.'

Nearly four years later, and a couple of weeks after the fall of Baghdad, I visited New York. The city was battling to conceal its triumphalism. Even among Manhattan's liberal

215

intelligentsia, which, from the start, has disclaimed the war in Iraq as belonging to people like backwater Pennsylvanians, the feeling of smugness was difficult to contain.

I asked an old friend about her abiding memory of the day Baghdad fell.

'I'm ashamed to admit it,' she said, with the liberal's obligatory preface of self-reflective distance, 'but I thought to myself, "even now that we have gone to war twice, they're too inept to launch one tiny terrorist attack on American soil."'

The Sunday edition of the *New York Times* lay on the table between us. The front page of its 'week in review' section led with a story about America's military supremacy. There was no longer an arms race, the article declared. 'Everyone else is so far behind the US, nobody is bothering to try to catch up.' The Iraqi air force, it went on to point out, did not dare put a single fighter in the air for the duration of the war.

I talked to another acquaintance about the CNN moment when the statue of Saddam was pulled to the ground and smashed to pieces.

'That was not a symbol of liberation,' I said. 'It was just a bunch of American soldiers and a few excitable teenagers bashing a piece of metal. The real image of the fall of Baghdad is looting and mayhem.'

'Does it really matter?' she replied. 'The point is that anti-American regimes are crapping themselves. For the first time since 9/11, I feel safe.'

At a flea market in Brooklyn, a vendor was selling a brand-new T-shirt. It sported a cartoon image of a crestfallen Saddam. Below the image, in huge black letters, a caption: 'Loser'.

Despite its prided sense of irony, it seemed that many New Yorkers really believed, with conviction and credulity, that America was safe because it could kill anyone, anytime, anywhere, under any circumstances.

In the immediate aftermath of the war, there were some superficial signs that New York's smugness was justified. In Iran, members of the country's conservative old guard began talking publicly, for the first time since the Islamic revolution in 1979, of détente with America. In Syria, a fawning president told US Secretary of State Colin Powell that his government would root out Syrian-based supporters of Palestinian terror. Even the maniacal little regime of North Korea seemed, on a good day at any rate, to be talking sense about nuclear weapons.

Yet for those of us who believe that the suicide of the American empire would cause a great deal of trouble for us all, the smugness of the superpower's most liberal city is cause for alarm. It is almost too prosaic to point out that a global empire is a helluva big place, much too big to rule by F-15 bombers. There will always be too many anytimes, anywheres and any circumstances.

Equally prosaic is that while bombers can break things, they cannot fix them. And the Bush administration is not going to be much of a fixer. It plans to spend a paltry $1.7 billion on the reconstruction of Iraq, leaving behind only a large military base in nearby Jordan – packed with F-15s and other goodies.

Leaving New York, it appeared to me that the city had a lot to learn about empires and safety. And it seemed to have forgotten that hubris always ends badly.

THE COURTS

Generous judgment instils stigma

24 April 2007

Something disturbing happened in the Constitutional Court earlier this month. Something went wrong in the case of NM and others v Charlene Smith, Patricia de Lille and another. That two judges dissented from the majority opinion is unremarkable in itself; disagreement about constitutional interpretation is what the court's work is about. But the dispute here was not about the interpretation of the law. In her dissent, Kate O'Regan argued that the ruling her colleagues handed down was inconsistent with the facts of the case. That is utterly unprecedented. For the first time, the court dragged itself beyond the boundaries of its specialist role and fought over matters that are rightly settled in the lower courts. What happened?

In 1999, several HIV-positive people were recruited to participate in an antiretroviral drug trial at the University of Pretoria. Soon after its commencement, some of the volunteers voiced serious concerns about the trial. Parliamentarian Patricia de Lille became involved in their plight. The university appointed an independent commission of inquiry. At the inquiry, the complainants withdrew their allegations, and the subsequent Strauss Report concluded in 2001 that the university had done no wrong.

Later that year, De Lille commissioned Charlene Smith to write her biography. Smith read De Lille's copy of the Strauss Report. It named three of the HIV-positive women who had complained about the trial. What Smith did not know is that the women had consented to testify at the inquiry on condition that their names were not made public. That information was contained in an annexure of the Strauss Report, but the report had been distributed without its annexure.

When Smith's biography of De Lille appeared, the names of the three HIV-positive women were in it. The doctor who ran the drug trial read the book and informed the three women of the appearance of their names. They sued for violation of privacy, dignity and psychological integrity. They said word of their HIV status had gotten out in the shack settlement in which they lived and they had suffered horrific prejudice.

Here is where the court split on matters of fact. O'Regan argued that Smith and De Lille could not reasonably have known that the women required their names to be concealed. If anyone was negligent, she argued, it was those who distributed the Strauss Report without its annexure. The university, a reputable source, had already published the women's names. To insist that a journalist re-investigate the veracity of information published by reputable sources, O'Regan argued, 'would result in unacceptable burdens being imposed on the dissemination of information and have a significantly deleterious effect on freedom of speech.'

The majority found the facts to be very different. They argued that Smith and De Lille knew that the three women wanted their names concealed and deliberately violated their privacy. Alternatively, they knew it was very likely that the women had not given their consent and published their names in reckless disregard of that likelihood.

The majority's finding is pretty bracing. Not even the three women's counsel argued that Smith and De Lille intended to violate their clients' privacy. Why was the court the only one to see intent?

One can only speculate. The fact that the applicants were among the most vulnerable South Africans imaginable probably played its part. They were poor women, lived in shacks, and were HIV positive. And they had been badly hurt. At a raw emotional level, the court must have struggled with the prospect of ruling against them.

The majority could have stuck to O'Regan's version of the facts if it had argued that Smith had violated the applicants' privacy because of negligence rather than intent. But there was a problem here. Under the common law, violation of privacy because of negligence is not liable. To award damages on the grounds of negligence, the court would have had to develop the common law. For whatever reason, they did not want to go there. They were thus faced with an uncomfortable choice. Either find against the three women, or cajole the facts into singing the right tune. I think the court chose the latter.

That they did so is unfortunate and not only for the law. In their haste to side with the meek, I believe the court has inadvertently entrenched AIDS stigma.

One of the things at the core of AIDS stigma is a feeling

of self-loathing in those who suffer it. To have internalised stigma is to persecute yourself incessantly. And you scan the world looking for signs that the persecution you feel within is mirrored from without, that everyone who looks at you sees inside your body and soul and feels disgust.

I am not suggesting that stigma exists only in the imaginations of the stigmatised. That is patently absurd. But the persecution felt by those in the depths of stigmatisation has a special occult quality to it. That is why across South Africa thousands of people with AIDS believe they have been bewitched. AIDS and witchcraft are natural bedfellows: the coupling of sickness and a sense of persecution is precisely the cocktail that has always fuelled feelings of bewitchment.

The urgent task of South Africa's leaders is to break the cycle of mythology and fear. The Constitutional Court has done the very opposite. Read the majority's judgment and you will find that both its tone and its strange logic carry something of the spirit of bewitchment. What was at very worst a negligent act of omission on the part of a journalist and a politician the court transforms into menacing intent to do ill. And the power of Smith's and De Lille's intent also takes on an almost occult power. The court tells that the three women suffered terrible prejudice as a result of their names being published: one attempted suicide, another withdrew into herself, the third lived in fear that her family would discover her status. Perhaps it is true that all of this pain was caused by the publication of the names, but the court did not deem it necessary to show empirical, causal connections. Given the sense of the occult that shrouds AIDS, it should have. The tone of the judgment suggests that there is no need to show causal connections; that the very fact of having your name revealed will as a matter of fate cause an orgy of loathing and violence to come down on your head.

If I arrived in South Africa for the first time and read the court's judgment, I would not test for HIV in this country. I would feel safer not knowing my status.

Something went wrong on Constitution Hill.

Seizing the sense behind the law

10 April, 2007

The Constitutional Court is seldom more interesting than when it is divided. In Mohunram v The National Director of Public Prosecutions, handed down last month, the judges were as close to evenly split as they can be – six to five. The question that divided them is one that is increasingly coming to define our national identity: what measure of pain is the state permitted to inflict upon wrongdoers in its quest to contain crime?

The matter at hand was how aggressive asset forfeiture can get before it violates the right to property. Kumarnath Mohunram was a small-town businessman from Vryheid. From one part of his commercial premises he ran a glass and aluminium business. From the other he ran 57 gambling machines. In 2001, he was charged with running a casino without a licence. Under criminal law, he paid R88 500 in admission of guilt fines. His gambling machines, worth R285 000, were seized and destroyed.

So much for the criminal law. Next, the public prosecutor launched a civil case against Mohunram under South Africa's asset forfeiture law. Using the civil evidentiary threshold of balance of probabilities, rather than the

226

more challenging criminal threshold of reasonable doubt, the law permits the state to confiscate property used to commit a crime, and assets deemed to be proceeds of crime. The civil court ordered the forfeiture of Mohunram's premises, including the part from which he ran his legitimate business, on the grounds that they had been used as instruments of crime.

The matter that divided the Constitutional Court was whether this robust use of asset forfeiture law violated Mohunram's right to property. The majority said that it did. In two separate judgments, Dikgang Moseneke and Albie Sachs said that the purpose of asset forfeiture law was to go after big fish: racketeering, extortion, large-scale money laundering. Gutting a minnow like Mohunram strayed too far from the law's purpose. Besides, the criminal law had already dealt with him. Nailing him again with the civil law was gratuitous, a greedy lunge for a bigger piece of him.

The minority judgment, penned by acting Constitutional Court judge Belinda van Heerden, begged to differ. The statute states quite clearly, she argued, that asset forfeiture's reach extends beyond organised crime. It explicitly lists illegal gambling as an offence to which forfeiture applies. And among the express purposes of forfeiture is to deter people from using their property as instruments of crime. Mohunram, she argued, found himself slap-bang in the centre of the law's target.

Van Heerden's judgment is a model of clarity. It gives the prosecution service a crisp interpretation of the law, and thus an easy guide from which to conduct its business. The two judgments that constitute the majority are messy and opaque: they pass on to the prosecution and the lower courts a great deal of confusion.

Yet if Moseneke's and Sachs's judgments are not as elegant as Van Heerden's, they are far wiser, for they have gone some way in teaching a thoughtless legislature something about law-drafting.

It is instructive to recall the context that gave birth to civil asset forfeiture. It of course has different roots in different jurisdictions, but one of the origins of the current fashion can be traced to March 1982 when a man named Pio La Torre, head of the Communist Party in Sicily, appealed to Italy's parliament to make it possible to confiscate the assets of known mafiosi if it could be shown that they were acquired with proceeds of crime.

The context was this: the Mafia controlled Sicily's construction industry and most of its capital markets. Using these instruments, they had effectively taken control of the island's public policy, from urban design to policing. Public officials who crossed them were systematically murdered. If only, La Torre thought aloud, we could follow the money trail from drugs and racketeering to the construction companies and the banks; and if only we could bring these companies and banks down, we could transfer control of public policy back to democratic institutions. Weeks after he made his appeal, La Torre was assassinated.

It was in these circumstances – a brazen usurpation of state functions by criminal empires effectively untouchable by criminal prosecution – that Italy began to take seriously the prospect of civil forfeiture.

By the time South Africa came to contemplate forfeiture,

it was so much in fashion it was considered pretty much obligatory. Organised crime was the greatest threat to fledging democratic states like ours, we were told. If we do not want public policy to be hijacked the way it was in Sicily, we need state-of-the-art enforcement.

The justice department drafted the law in the late 1990s. At precisely that time, the legislature had begun in earnest to throw the kitchen sink at South Africa's crime wave. It had just passed a sentencing law that would dramatically inflate the time felons spent in jail; it had also passed an extraordinarily harsh new bail law. Parliament was behaving like the figure in a music box; open its lid and it would pop up and sing for more punishment.

Handed yet another weapon – asset forfeiture – the legislature couldn't help itself. The title of the Act sticks close to the original purpose of asset forfeiture: 'to introduce measures to combat organised crime, money laundering and criminal gang activities.' Yet by the time the drafters got round to the meat of the legislation, they had, in their excitement, forgotten all about its purpose. They chucked in every crime they could think of, including any offence that carries a jail sentence of more than a year.

Van Heerden read the statute with faultless rigour. The title of the Act, she said, is 'incorrect' and 'unfortunate', since 'the wording of the Act as a whole makes it clear that its ambit is NOT in fact limited to so-called organised criminal offences'.

Moseneke and Sachs chose another path: hold on, they told the legislature. You may have forgotten the title of your own statute by the time you'd finished writing it, but we're going to hold you to it nonetheless. You can list as many crimes as you like, but unless the crime in question 'has some rational link … with racketeering, money laundering and criminal gang activities …' asset forfeiture runs the risk of being disproportionate and thus unconstitutional. Hence, Mohunram keeps his property.

Unfortunately, it is sloppy law. Just a few months ago, the Constitutional Court okayed forfeiture proceedings against a lone entrepreneur who manufactured tik. No evidence was produced that he was a member of an organised syndicate, a racketeer, or a gang member. Yet the court ruled that civil forfeiture was constitutionally permissible.

It has thus created a wide grey zone in which prosecutors cannot know whether their actions are permissible. Prosecutors will thus make narrow and conservative choices. But perhaps that is a good thing. The legislature of the late 1990s was unhinged. It didn't have the means to make our justice system work better. So it did the one thing it could do: rip the guts out of the few wrongdoers who are caught. That's the task to which it almost turned asset forfeiture. But that is not what asset forfeiture is for.

Two judgments that show a new light, an old shadow

17 January 2006

Judges are at their most interesting both when they are strong and when they are weak. They are interesting when they show robustness and creativity, and they are equally interesting when they show inconsistency. For it is when judges speak in two voices, having meant to speak only in one, that the relationship between the law and the human beings who interpret it is stripped bare.

During the course of 2005, the Constitutional Court faced two cases in which its judges had to put thought to questions of sexual morality. In the more famous of the two, Minister of Home Affairs v Fourie, an exuberant judgment which unabashedly celebrated sexual diversity, the court recognised gay marriage. Yet nine months earlier, in Volks v Robinson, the court, positively Victorian in its priggishness, denied maintenance rights to life partners who are not married.

It is not obvious at first blush that there is any discrepancy between these two judgments. I wish to show, however, that there is, and that what the discrepancy reveals is a court possessed by a squeamish middle-class morality and a concomitant obtuseness in the face of the tough politics of modern South African sexuality.

231

The Fourie judgment is uncompromising in its refusal to reduce marriage to any particular moralistic conception. Marriage, Justice Albie Sachs writes on behalf of a unanimous court, has outgrown 'its earlier purpose in the common law of legitimising sexual relations and securing succession of legitimate heirs to family property'. Nor can marriage be defined as the institution through which human beings procreate. This, the court argues, would be 'deeply demeaning to couples ... incapable of procreating ... [and] to adoptive parents ... It is even demeaning of a couple who voluntarily decide not to have children or sexual relations with one another ...' Nor can marriage be reduced to any biblical injunction for 'it would be out of order to employ the religious sentiments of some as a guide to the constitutional rights of others'.

In short, marriage means nothing over and beyond the rights and interests of those who choose to enter into the institution. Chief among those rights is the facility to affirm publicly one's union to another human being, and to fall back on state regulation when that union is in trouble. To deny these rights to same-sex couples is to reinforce 'the wounding notion that they are to be treated as biological oddities, as failed or lapsed human beings ...'

There is a sense in which the Fourie judgment is too good to be true; so sparkling and bathed in sunlight that one finds oneself searching for the shadows. It is positively radical in its doggedness that no priest and no moralist can lay exclusive claim to the meaning of a life union between two people. It is entirely at ease with the idea that life unions are the product of an irreducible human creativity, that to punish or curtail this creativity in the name of received doctrine is unacceptable. As one reads, one finds oneself wondering whether the court can possibly be as uninhibited as it claims, whether it has really banished all moralistic predilections in regard to its reading of the relationship between sexual union and law.

And indeed, the court's inhibitions are on display, although not in the same judgment. To find them, one must turn to Volks v Robinson. The central issue in Volks is this: a heterosexual couple lives a long stretch of their lives together under the same roof, in financial and emotional interdependence. The breadwinner dies. If the couple is married, the Maintenance Act gives the survivor the right to claim maintenance from the deceased estate. If the couple isn't married, she has no such right. The constitutional question raised in Volks is whether the law discriminates against her on the grounds that she is unmarried.

The majority said no. South Africa, Justice Sandile Ngcobo argued in one of two majority judgments, has a constitutional obligation to protect marriage. It does not frown on other forms of union, but it protects marriage. To impose the legal consequences of marriage on those who have not chosen it is to 'undermine … the nature of the agreement inherent in marriage', indeed, is to 'undermine the right freely to marry'. Finding in favour of Volks, Ngcobo is saying, would empty marriage of its content, rendering the public exchange of vows meaningless.

How does this judgment compare to Fourie? The first thing to point out is not so much a discrepancy as a shift in perspective. The spirit of Fourie is strikingly anti-teleological: its hallmark is its insistence that life unions need not and ought not conform to any received doctrine. Yet Volks is all about sexual doctrine. The court's majority judgments are clearly grounded on the doctrine that the unions of those who publicly vow to a lifelong, monogamous commitment must be privileged over those who do not.

'So what?' you may reply. Heterosexual couples have always had the choice to marry; gay couples haven't. Unmarried heterosexuals have never been subject to state-sanctioned persecution; homosexuals have. If heterosexual couples find themselves excluded from the rights of marriage, it is their choice.

This argument is in fact wrong. Like any other institution, marriage has a material foundation: it works when it has the resources to back it, and it fails when those resources are absent. There was perhaps a time, several generations ago, when the vast majority of young South African women, although unable to earn an independent wage, nonetheless grew up in self-supporting households. And they assumed, when they reached adulthood, that the self-supporting households of their parents would still be there 10 or 20 years later. As any South African anthropologist familiar with early twentieth century research will tell you, most women married, but a surprisingly large number, even in the most traditional communities, divorced. They returned to their parents' homes, where they lived comfortable lives as single, often sexually active, women. They were not beholden to estranged husbands or defeated marriages because they would not starve if they left them.

Today, a significant minority of young South African women reach adulthood with access neither to jobs nor to self-supporting households. For them, bonds of love mingle with tacit financial transactions. A man is their only possible access to income. Many do not marry because their partners neither want nor need that commitment. Such women are financially dependent on their partners and yet utterly unprotected. Their predicament is neither chosen nor a symptom of moral failing: it is built into the structure of contemporary South African life. The Constitutional Court was given the opportunity to protect them, but did not.

Faced with gay couples, the court is wonderfully alive to the fact that institutions must be flexible in the face of the diversity of human needs. Yet faced with the needs, the interests and the life strategies of those for whom the choice to marry is as empty as it is formal, the court offers only its stern Victorian back.

Courts can't write policy,
but they can get politicians to

14 November 2005

Is it possible to use constitutional law to remedy systemic dysfunctions in governance? Do judges have the authority and the expertise to tell government how to make very hard political choices and how to fix complicated administrative problems?

These questions are raised in tantalising fashion in a case called Prison Care and Support Network v the Government, which was put on the Cape High Court roll this spring. The litigants' first objective is to have the courts declare that levels of prison overcrowding are constitutionally unacceptable. This is the least interesting aspect of the case. Currently, South African prisons on average house one inmate for every 2.4 square metres of floor space, a situation which violates minimum conditions of detention even by the most slovenly standards.

Far more interesting is the remedy the litigants are seeking. They want the courts to order government to design a wide-ranging programme of criminal justice reform – from reducing unnecessary arrests, to reviewing sentencing legislation, to building prisons – and to have the courts oversee the implementation of this programme. Are the litigants asking too much of constitutional law? Are they asking for the offices of the justice, correctional services and public works ministers to be moved into a judge's chambers?

The causes of prison overcrowding are not hard to grasp. Jail space is a scarce resource. In the mid-1990s, we began to forget that. We swelled the ranks of our prison population – primarily by increasing the severity of sentences and narrowing the space for early releases – without a thought to where we were going to house inmates.

The solution, too, is conceptually simple. We need to build more prison space than we currently are, send fewer people to jail, and reverse the trend of sending them there for longer and longer periods. How many people we choose to imprison must be informed by the amount of prison space we are prepared to make available.

Conceptually simple, maybe, but politically difficult. It costs about R650 million to build a new facility with a capacity to house 3 000 inmates. At current rates of overcrowding, government would have to build 14 such prisons just to bring inmate volumes back to capacity. Are the courts to order government to crowd out spending on housing or social grants in order to build prisons? The other remedies are no easier. Shortening prison sentences is unlikely to trigger an increase in crime, but it will provoke popular doubt about the state's willingness to protect its citizens from harm. Can courts order the government to weaken its own legitimacy in the eyes of its electorate?

The litigants are surely aware of how tough the issues are. I doubt whether they are sufficiently starry-eyed to believe that a judge is going to attempt to rewrite criminal justice policy on the back of a yellow legal pad. What the litigants do know, however, is that they are taking government on a long journey. The case is likely to make its way to Bloemfontein and then to the Constitutional Court. In the course of that journey, government is going to have to think about prison overcrowding, and it will have to commit its thoughts to paper. From bail and parole policy, to sentencing legislation, to the use of arrests, to prison-building plans, government will have to run its mind across the gamut of the criminal justice system with a view to addressing chronic prison overcrowding. And it will have to show that it has thought reasonably about these matters.

The litigants hope that in the end the courts will be able to hand down a fairly detailed order, embodying meaningful institutional reform, lifted entirely from the government's affidavits. This is, incidentally, precisely what happened in the famous nevirapine case in 2002. At the beginning of the High Court case, the government's affidavits admitted nothing. By the end of the Constitutional Court case, it had committed itself to making nevirapine available to every HIV-positive expectant mother. The court order reflected government's own stated commitments.

The answer to the question – is it possible to use constitutional law to remedy systemic dysfunctions in governance? – is a complicated yes. It is not necessary for judges to redesign institutions on the back of a legal pad, nor to make tough political choices on government's behalf. On the contrary, their role is to remind politicians that the tough choices are their own – that it is not acceptable, for instance, to run a criminal justice system as if prison space is unlimited.

When serving any time amounts to cruel and unusual punishment

17 October 2005

Two months ago, writing on behalf of a three-person Supreme Court of Appeal bench, Judge Mohamed Navsa cut short the sentence of a convict before she had served half her prison time. He did so on the grounds that serving the remainder of her sentence would probably kill her. Judge Navsa has opened a Pandora's Box, for if judges are going to begin scrutinising the discrepancy between the punishment courts prescribe and the actual conditions under which punishment is served, we are quickly going to discover that, in their current state, our prisons simply do not belong in South Africa's legal order.

The case was that of Magida v State. In 1999, Memory Magida, a 26-year-old mother, was charged with 99 counts of cheque fraud. While awaiting trial in jail she contracted tuberculosis. In 2001, she was sentenced to an effective five-and-a-half years in prison. Early in her sentence, she fell ill with shingles and thrush. She took an HIV test and discovered that she had full-blown AIDS.

Magida appealed against her sentence, partly on the grounds that if she remained in jail she would soon die.

She was released on bail, pending her appeal. In the meantime, she enrolled in a government-sponsored anti-retroviral treatment programme at Groote Schuur Hospital. Her health improved considerably. Antiretro-virals (ARVs) were unavailable to her in prison. If she went back, she would have to terminate treatment.

Cape High Court judges John Hlope and Beverly Franks dismissed Magida's appeal with unconcealed contempt. They were, they wrote, 'not aware of any good authority for the view that if someone is HIV positive he or she may get away with murder.'

Magida appealed again, this time to Bloemfontein, where her case was heard by Navsa and two colleagues. They overturned Hlope's and Franks's order and resentenced Magida to precisely the time she had already served, thus effectively setting her free. Although not in so many words, they argued that Magida had been sentenced to five-and-a-half years, rather than to death, and that confining her to a place where she would grow sick and die was unjust.

Aside from the absence of ARVs in prison, Navsa pointed out in his judgment, 'her diet in prison and a lack of the range of necessary vitamins are not conducive to combating her present condition ... In her own words: "My immune system crashed."'

The repercussions of this judgment are serious. More than 1 600 South African prisoners died in custody of natural causes last year, most of them almost certainly from AIDS. How many died years before they might have because our prisons are overcrowded, prone to contagion, and have nutritional and medical systems incapable of tending to the ill? How many of those 1 600 were, according to the rubric of the Supreme Court of Appeal's judgment, serving unjust sentences?

The implications of the judgment go beyond the question of AIDS. They speak to the general issue of the gap between punishment handed down and actual punishment experienced. Were an openly gay man to show that he has a 90% chance of being raped in prison, or a first-time offender to show that he is certain to be severely beaten, would the actual sentence he serves not be unacceptably more severe than the sentence handed down?

Navsa's judgment was in fact reasonably cautious. Other South African judges have been a good deal more severe. In 2003, for instance, Eastern Cape High Court Judge Clive Plasket was confronted with a series of cases in which juveniles had been sentenced to serve time in a reform school. The province had no reform schools and the juveniles were housed in police cells and prisons.

Plasket freed them on the grounds that the State was unable to implement their sentences. Among the rights he argued had been violated, the most interesting was the right to a fair trial. The notion of a fair trial, he said, 'must include the right not to be subjected to a sentence substantially more severe than the one imposed by the court.'

I am not suggesting that the judiciary is about to, or ought to, refuse to send anyone to jail. But we clearly have a serious problem. In their chronically overcrowded and violent state, South African prisons are not places our legal system envisages anyone spending time. It is a problem for the rule of law, for criminal justice, and, indeed, for our sense of who we are. It was Nelson Mandela who said that 'no-one truly knows a nation until one has been inside its jails'.

Court meets needs of homeless wanderers by a tortuous route

20 May 2005

There was a moment in the Constitutional Court in May 2000 which is difficult to forget. It was the famous case on the right to housing, The State v Grootboom. The government's counsel, Jeremy Gauntlet, told the court his client was slowly fulfilling its constitutional obligation, that in the long run everyone would be housed.

'In the long run,' then Constitutional Court President Arthur Chaskalson replied, citing John Maynard Keynes, 'we are all dead. What about people who are homeless here and now? Are you saying they must wander from place to place until they find land from which no-one will evict them …?'

It is an unpleasant moment for an advocate, to stand before a judge so eloquent and so very much on the side of the angels. Gauntlet was uncharacteristically stumped.

Yet eloquence can be a little too easy. Nearly five years later, the court was confronted with precisely the case about which Chaskalson had mused – a group of homeless people wandering from place to place, looking for land from which no-one would evict them – in the form of The President v Modderklip. While the order the court handed down earlier this month is to be applauded, the manner in which it got there was tortuous and inelegant, illustrating that the right to housing keeps haunting the court, that taming this right is inordinately tough.

The facts of the case are these: in the mid-1990s, several thousand people occupied a strip of municipal land on the East Rand, establishing what became known as the Chris Hani settlement. The municipality tore Chris Hani down in mid-2000 and about 400 of its residents moved their shacks to adjacent land which they thought was municipal property, but was in fact a privately owned farm. The owner, Braam Duvenhage, was granted an eviction order, which the occupiers of his farm ignored. By 2001, the settlement had grown to 40 000 people.

Duvenhage obtained a writ of execution, and the sheriff was requested to execute. She insisted that Duvenhage put down a deposit of R1.8 million to cover the eviction costs. He refused. He went to the presidency, which referred him to the Department of Land Affairs, which referred him to the Housing Department, which did not respond. Finally, Duvenhage went to court.

When the case reached the Supreme Court of Appeal, it ruled that in failing to provide the occupiers with land, the state had both breached their right to adequate housing and Duvenhage's property rights. A powerful and far-reaching implication was that the state violated Duvenhage's rights in the very process of violating the occupiers' rights. It ordered that land be made available to the occupiers and that Duvenhage be paid damages.

The Constitutional Court was never going to be comfortable with this reasoning. It knew the Supreme Court of Appeal's decision was right, that unless the state provided the occupiers with land, they would, in Chaskalson's words of May 2000, 'wander from place to place', serially invading the land of others, simply to put roofs over their heads.

Yet the Constitutional Court decided several years ago that it is unlikely ever to interpret the right to housing to mean that particular individuals can access accommodation on demand. It is prepared to rule that the state set aside money to house the homeless as an abstract category, but not that this particular homeless person be given that piece of land. The court is, quite simply, scared of a cascade, and thus of imposing on the state an obligation it cannot meet.

So what to do in the Modderklip case? The court knew it had to order the state to find land for the occupiers, but it didn't want to say that their right to housing had been violated.

In the end, the judges performed an ungainly feat. Extraordinarily, they short-circuited both the right to housing and property and decided the matter on an altogether different basis. They argued what had been violated was Duvenhage's right to have a dispute resolved by a court, and that the only resolution consistent with the maintenance of social order and the rule of law was to provide the occupiers with alternative land.

To be sure, it is a powerful, commendable outcome, but the journey was not pretty. When Chaskalson conjured an image of eternal wanderers in May 2000, he

245

imagined them as possessors of a constitutional right that had been violated. That spectacle has proved too difficult for the court to contemplate. It is easier to deal with the wanderers, it seems, as a threat to social order.

Judges shrug in bemusement

23 March 2004

In 2003, parliament chose to disenfranchise all prisoners serving a jail sentence without the option of a fine in the following year's national elections. Nicro, the prisoners' aid organisation, contested the legislation in the Constitutional Court and won. Much of the country was appalled by the court's decision.

Much of South Africa greeted the Constitutional Court's decision to allow all prisoners to vote on 14 April with disgruntled resignation. When the judgment was handed down, President Thabo Mbeki said he did not think it right that all prisoners vote, but that the court's decision must be respected.

During the following week, columnists and letter-writers in just about every national daily expressed disgust that rapists and murderers would vote; like Mbeki, though, they mostly added that the court's judgment ought to be respected. It appears that the whole country was reluctantly humouring what it took to be the court's wrong-headedness.

The court has, in fact, been misunderstood. At no point does its majority judgment say there are no good reasons to disenfranchise people serving time for serious crimes. On the contrary, it implies that there might be very good reasons. It is just that government failed to bring any to court. Government's submission was spectacularly shoddy. It missed the entire point of constitutional argument.

The court's majority position is not a symptom of its liberalism. It is, rather, an expression of its seriousness, of its belief that taking away the rights of citizens is a grave matter, and should never be done in the absence of reasoned debate.

Whenever policy or legislation limits a constitutional right – in this case, the right to vote – there is a well-established constitutional onus that government must fulfil. First, it must say to what purpose it is limiting the right, and convince the court that the limitation is justifiable in an open and democratic society. Beyond that, government must argue convincingly that limiting the right is proportional to its purpose, that it is not, so to speak, using a shotgun to kill an ant.

If government had taken this test seriously, we would have been treated to a long-overdue debate about the relationship between imprisonment and democracy.

What was government's purpose when it decided to disenfranchise those serving prison sentences without the option of a fine? Was it to deter others from committing crimes? Was it salutary – a punitive lesson in the responsibilities of citizenship? Or was it about retribution, about hurting criminals with as many weapons as we can find? Or was it, alternatively, just an intuitive moral response; a belief that those who have committed a serious crime have robbed themselves of their moral agency and made themselves into outcasts; that they do not deserve to choose who governs them?

These are rival purposes. They are not alike. And it is not self-evident that all or any require limiting the franchise. Democracy is the foundation of the South African State's legitimacy. Is it right to truncate democracy in order to punish, or to teach, or to get retribution? These are not easy questions. To answer them, we need to reason.

Government neither asked nor answered these questions. In his affidavit, Home Affairs Director-General Barry Gilder attempted to short-circuit the entire debate with a bizarre claim. He argued that government had not denied anyone the right to vote. It had merely refused to make special voting arrangements for those serving prison sentences without the option of a fine.

There were several categories of people who would not be able to make it to the polls on 14 April, Gilder argued: prisoners who would have been free if they could have afforded the option of paying a fine; the elderly, the disabled and the infirm; people who could not go to their voting districts on 14 April because of duties connected to the elections.

Special voting, Gilder argued, places strain on the Independent Electoral Commission's logistical and financial capacity. It would not be fair to devote resources for criminals to vote, if similar provision could not be made for people who could not get to the polls due to no fault of their own.

'In a country in which crime is a major problem,' Gilder argued, '... it would be highly insensitive, and indeed irresponsible, to say to law-abiding citizens that some of the resources which could have been utilised to ameliorate the effect of the obligation to get themselves to their voting stations have been diverted to those who have infringed their rights.'

Gilder's argument was self-evidently spurious. Arrangements had already been made for unsentenced prisoners, as well as those incarcerated because they could not pay their fines, to register and vote in every prison across the country. The infrastructure for all prisoners to vote was in place anyway. The notion that the elderly and the infirm would be disadvantaged if bad people voted was no more than sentimental, populist polemic. As a contribution to the constitutional exercise of rights limitation it was valueless.

The court shrugged its shoulders in bemusement. It complained that people should not be 'left guessing' about why prisoners had been disenfranchised. It pointed wistfully to a court case in Canada in 2002 which, in its view, had taken the question of prisoner disenfranchisement seriously.

The Canadian government had disenfranchised convicts sentenced to two years or more in prison. In contrast to Gilder's affidavit, it offered two crisp reasons: first, to enhance respect for the rule of law; and second, to provide additional punishment for people who have committed serious crimes.

The Supreme Court of Canada was split five to four on its decision. The majority, which ruled against the government, called the legislation 'a façade of rhetoric'. It accused the government of 'jeopardising its claims to representative democracy' and of 'eroding the basis of its right to convict and punish law-breakers'.

'Common sense,' the minority replied dryly, 'dictates that social condemnation of criminal activity and a desire to promote civic responsibility are reflected in the disenfranchisement of those who have committed serious crimes.'

The South African Constitutional Court looked longingly to Canada to demonstrate what a serious debate on disenfranchisement might have looked like. In its stiffly polite manner, it was telling government that it is not good enough to bring cheap rhetoric about old and disabled people. The issue is too serious for that.

Farewell to a sparkling maverick

5 December 2002

Beyond the gushing platitudes that are customarily showered on a veteran judge when he hangs up his robes, what, in particular, has the Constitutional Court lost with the retirement of Johann Kriegler?

The court has been robbed of a genuine maverick. In the current South African context, in which public debate on the judiciary is arid and lazy, the depth of that loss is not immediately apparent.

I mean 'maverick' in the most sparkling sense of the term: a judge who relentlessly interrogates his own prejudices, an unfalteringly independent thinker, and, above all, an utterly unpredictable jurist.

Kriegler first revealed the extent of his unpredictability in 1997, in The President v Hugo. Nelson Mandela had issued a presidential pardon for all female prisoners with children under the age of 12. Hugo, a prisoner and a father, had contested the pardon on the grounds that it discriminated against men.

Kriegler argued that the women should remain locked up. He said that Mandela's pardon gave force to the prejudice that women are primary child minders, and that that prejudice was at the heart of the oppression of women.

The judgment would have been unremarkable had it been penned by a left-wing academic or a gender activist. Kriegler, though, had cut his teeth in one of the most conservative jurisprudential traditions on the planet. Yet he revealed himself to be a radical idealist, one who believed that constitutional law could be enlisted as a tool in one of the most ambitious egalitarian projects of our times.

Equally remarkable was Kriegler's judgment in the famous Fedsure case, where the Johannesburg Council quadrupled Sandton property rates in order to redistribute funds to poorer parts of the city.

The law upon which the council based its action was carelessly worded, and Arthur Chaskalson, a strict letter-of-the-law jurist, had little compunction in ruling against the council. Kriegler, however, was not going to allow poor legislative draftsmanship to get in his way. He argued that one of the fundamental purposes of post-apartheid local government was to redress urban inequality, and he interpreted the wording of the law with a degree of imaginative licence that raised eyebrows.

The weight of his intellectual authority prompted half the judges to go with him, and the court was split down the middle.

Perhaps most interesting of all, Kriegler penned the most sharply antilibertarian judgment the Constitutional Court has handed down, The State v Dlamini. He argued that an accused may be denied bail, and thus his liberty, not because of anything he might do, but because his release is likely to prompt vigilante action.

The judgment was striking because Kriegler is a renowned civil libertarian. He demonstrated – distastefully, to my mind, but that is not the point here – that even his most cherished principles ought to be re-examined in each and every situation.

Why does any of this matter? Why is a rigorous maverick important?

In the current South African context, debate about constitutional jurisprudence has been reduced to a single, stale question: is the judge scared of the executive? Is he a lapdog or a bulldog?

Things are infinitely subtler than that. Yes, courage in the face of a strong, often intolerant executive is crucial, but a million other factors shape the character of a court. Judges are intellectuals. Their job is to interpret the meaning of a document – the Constitution – and unless we are prepared to dismiss them as spineless absconders from the heart of their profession, we must assume that they do so with seriousness and integrity.

Different jurists bring different intellectual dispositions to their work. A judge like Arthur Chaskalson strives to develop a comprehensive jurisprudence, a set of carefully honed principles that can be applied to every case. That is a good quality in a chief justice; a court should have a rigorous and consistent philosophy.

But it has its downsides too, especially when the chief justice is intellectually formidable. An intellectually dominant 'totaliser' holds the danger of lulling a court, of allowing it to settle into a set of prejudices to which it slowly becomes blind.

That is one good reason why Constitutional Court judges

should not be appointed for life; like everything else in the world, courts become stale. It is also a good reason why every court needs a respected maverick, a jurist who is relentless in unsettling prejudices, who is prepared to re-examine everything all over again, at the onset of every case.

The court has lost its maverick, the one who unsettles the settled, who prods the complacent.

A court with no stomach
for flesh and blood

24 October 2002

The Constitutional Court's recent decision to uphold South Africa's prohibition of commercial sex reveals a great deal about the court, and much of what is revealed comes as a surprise.

I am not talking about the things that have preoccupied judiciary-watchers in recent years: the court's alleged squeamishness in taking on powerful political interests, or its fear of becoming marginalised. I am talking about its moral philosophy, its views on how a human life ought to be lived and on when it is legitimate for the state to interfere with the personal choices people make.

Here, the court has revealed itself to be sharply illiberal and surprisingly paternalistic.

One of the exercises the court undertook before arriving at its decision was to test whether the prohibition of sex work violates prostitutes' right to dignity. It does not, the court concluded, in a section of the judgment endorsed by all 11 judges. 'Our Constitution values the fundamental dignity of the human body,' they argued. The body is 'not something to be commodified ... The dignity of prostitutes is diminished, not by [the law that

256

criminalises commercial sex] but by their engaging in commercial sex work. The very character of the work they undertake devalues the respect that the Constitution regards as inherent in the human body.'

With these words, the court entered murky territory. It implied that there are things we do to our own bodies, harms we inflict on ourselves, and not on others, that might not pass constitutional muster. What is it that justifies a constitution poking its nose that far into the interior of a human life?

Recently, while on a journalistic assignment in a backwater town in Patagonia, I interviewed a group of prostitutes in a side street brothel. All were in their early twenties, all were migrant workers with homes more than a thousand kilometres away, and all were mothers. Between them, they offered two explanations for choosing commercial sex.

One is that they wanted their children to be educated and the men in their lives were never going to save enough money for a decent education. They needed, not just to work, but to leave home, in order to maintain control over the money they saved. The second reason is that the men in their lives did not allow them to work, and they valued the dignity of their independence more than the dignity of their bodies.

I have deliberately chosen examples of the most noble reasons for becoming a prostitute, but that is not the point. The point is that the women I interviewed understood something about moral philosophy that South Africa's Constitutional Court appears not to have understood: that sometimes people are forced to make tragic choices, tragic in the sense that you lose a piece of your dignity either way. You sacrifice the dignity of your body in order to secure the dignity of your offspring: you sacrifice the dignity of your body for the dignity of your independence.

The finest liberal philosophers of the twentieth century, like Isaiah Berlin (whom the court is fond of quoting), grounded their liberalism precisely in the idea of tragic choices. There are times, Berlin said, when you will lose something either way. Who has the authority, in tragic instances, to take away your right to choose? What constitution, and what government, knows better than you that the dignity that inheres in your body is more sacred than the education of your children?

So, the court might be right to say that commercial sex devalues the dignity inherent in the human body. And yet, strangely, it did not even entertain the prospect that criminalising prostitution might violate the dignity that inheres in making tragic choices.

I am not saying that this issue was decisive. The court may have acknowledged that the right to make tragic choices was being violated, and maintained the prohibition anyhow, on the grounds that the purpose behind the prohibition justified the limitation of the right to choose. But it did not do that. It took no cognisance at all of the most simple and poignant liberal argument.

Why not? Why was the court so thoroughly paternalistic? Because, in essence, the court has a vision of a society in which there will be no gender inequality, a society in which women will not face the choice of degrading their bodies to earn money.

That is touchingly quaint, but in the here and now, there are flesh-and-blood women who ought to have the right to choose which particular form of inequality they are prepared to stomach.

When everybody has a right to nothing at all

8 May 2002

For those in search of a riveting Friday afternoon, the Constitutional Court's premises in Braamfontein are not an obvious port of call. But for half an hour last Friday, the courtroom played host to an extraordinary public exchange, one that left the gallery entranced.

The man appearing before the court, Wim Trengove, is among the most respected jurists of his generation. While his demeanour was dressed in the deference and restraint that court protocol demands, and while his discourse was eloquent and passionate, rather than jarring, his indignation was difficult to conceal. In essence, he told the court that its interpretation of socioeconomic rights was hollowing out the Constitution, defying its express purposes, leaving it barren.

The case was the famous one about the administration of nevirapine in state hospitals. Trengove was not one of the two protagonists. Appearing as an amicus – a friend of the court – on behalf of the Community Law Centre and Idasa, his position gave him licence to conduct a free-wheeling assault on the court's thinking.

To understand his complaint, it is necessary to start

at the beginning, with exactly what the Constitution says about socioeconomic rights.

Take, for instance, section 26, the right to housing. Section 26(1) says that 'everyone has the right to have access to adequate housing'. Section 26(2) adds that 'the state must take reasonable ... measures within its available resources to achieve the progressive realisation of this right'.

Two years ago, in The State v Grootboom, the Constitutional Court told the world how it understood this right. It argued that 26(2) places severe restrictions on the right expressed in 26(1). Instead of arguing that socioeconomic rights place a duty on the state to provide specific services on demand, it said that such rights place a duty on the state to allocate its resources reasonably. So, in the Grootboom case, it said that the government's housing policy, which consisted only of a long-term brick-and-mortar programme, was unreasonable in the face of mass homelessness in the here and now. It ordered government to set aside a 'reasonable proportion' of its housing budget for short-term relief.

It is not difficult to see why the court chose to interpret 26(1) so conservatively. Beyond the trivially obvious point that providing housing, healthcare, food, water and social security for everyone in the here and now would decimate the fiscus, and beyond the equally obvious point that providing services piecemeal, on demand, would unravel rational planning, something more subtle and interesting was at stake.

Say the court was to ask itself whether government could afford to house the homeless. Essentially, it would have to open up the totality of government spending to review. It requires little empathy to see that this is a terrifying prospect for a judge. Beyond the spectacle of green-robed jurists buried under a daunting mountain of figures, there is something conceptual and philosophical at stake.

Allocating resources across a behemoth-like bureaucracy is no mean task. There are a thousand competing priorities; many are of equal importance. It is obvious that no one, two, or even ten ways is best. There comes a point when rival ways of distributing resources are incommensurable. The danger the court faces is one of clumsiness and obtuseness. The further it enmeshes itself in this, the stickiest of arenas, the greater the chance that it will ride roughshod over a painstakingly thoughtful allocation of resources.

Is it not better, then, to acknowledge that there are a thousand reasonable ways to juggle competing priorities? Is it not better to say: we will stop you when your allocation is unreasonable, but anything below that threshold is your business, not ours?

Trengove's response to this argument is disarmingly simple. This debate is all very well, he might reply, but, for better or for worse, those who wrote South Africa's Constitution have already resolved it. The Constitution has said plainly, in black and white, that socioeconomic rights are vested in individuals. What on earth can this mean other than that individuals can come to court to demand their rights? The way you have interpreted the Constitution, Trengove told the court, 'nobody has a right to anything in particular, and therefore, everyone has a right to nothing at all.'

'Are you saying,' Chief Justice Arthur Chaskalson asked with incredulity, 'that everyone should get a house?'

Well, not quite. The Constitution is animated by the values of dignity, equality and freedom. Section 26(1), the right to decent housing, means that anybody should be able to demand 'the minimum core' of the right to housing, defined as 'the minimum core necessary for a dignified human existence'.

'I haven't given thought to the exact content of "minimum core",' Trengove said, 'but in regard to 26(1) it at least includes a plot, rudimentary building materials, some basic services. Finding where the line should be drawn is difficult, but it is better than never meeting ...'

'Why do you say "never"?' Chaskalson interrupted.

'"Reasonable measures",' Trengove replied, 'gives the state such wide latitude that maybe everyone will get the bare minimum in 20 or 30 years. In the meantime, people will live and die with their constitutional rights in their hands.

'How can you expect the poorest of the poor to come here and debate whether it is better to spend R40 billion on arms than spend money on land?' With reasonableness as the benchmark, 'the big cases, backed by big lobbies, will succeed. But those for whom socioeconomic rights were created will not have a chance.'

'Would socioeconomic rights not be limited by cost?' Justice Richard Goldstone asked.

'Yes, cost is a factor,' Trengove replied. 'If the core is too expensive in some instances, limitation comes in. But at least it will be an issue of public debate.'

There lies the rub. The court is not sure it wants to be

the one to adjudicate over that public debate. It is, for reasons I have detailed above, pretty squeamish about opening up the fiscus to detailed review.

One must have some sympathy for this squeamishness. Trengove is asking the judiciary to play a heady, high-stakes game.

There are times when judiciaries have played this game with gusto. In the 1960s, West Germany's constitutional court ordered government to restructure the entire tertiary education system. It went so far as to scrutinise the fine print of university budgets, examining admissions one by one. But that was in a time, and in a country, where politics had been shamed by the Holocaust, and public culture expected judges to push politicians around. It is not clear that our public culture would, or even should, tolerate judges in a managerial role.

So, one must have sympathy with the Constitutional Court. But if Trengove is right, if the court has disregarded the most simple and profound constitutional charge, that rights vest in individuals, one should also be alive to the heavy price the court has paid.

AIDS

When AIDS treatment is viewed as collective racial humiliation

2 July 2007

More than 300 000 South Africans are on antiretroviral (ARV) treatment. More than two-thirds of them are women. Why? Where are the missing men? Why are they not coming forward? It is a very hard question, and I don't plan to do it justice here. Instead, I want to nibble at one neglected corner of an answer by telling the story of a single man.

I recently spent 18 months travelling to and from the town of Lusikisiki in the Eastern Cape, researching an ARV treatment programme there. At the beginning of the project, I hired an interpreter from an outlying village, a 30-year-old man whom I shall call Sizwe. He and I toured the clinics of the Lusikisiki district, speaking to many men and women on ARV treatment.

It soon became clear that what I was seeing through my eyes was very different to what Sizwe was seeing through his. I witnessed the miracle of a lifesaving drug. Everywhere we met people who, in the absence of ARVs, would have been dying or dead. Most associated their twice-daily treatment with continued life, with health, and with their attachment to those they loved.

What Sizwe saw, in contrast, were endless scores of black people dependent for their survival on Western drugs. 'Before going on this tour with you,' he told me, 'I knew of only six people who had died from AIDS. Now I see it is everywhere. Wherever we go, people are on drugs: people who cough, people who breathe cleanly, people with skin disease and people with clear skin. Whole villages, it seems, are on drugs. Does that mean everyone in my village is sick too? If we all tested for HIV, would the whole village end up taking these pills?'

Sizwe did not doubt for a moment that the meaning and the origins of the epidemic were political. 'Why is it a disease of blacks,' he asked, 'and not a disease of whites? And why did it come only after 1994? We have a saying in isiXhosa: when you see smoke in the sky, it means some people have been lighting a fire. It is not just there in the sky. There are people at the bottom.'

As for the spectacle of treatment itself, it was, for Sizwe, a source of humiliation. 'AIDS is a disease people are ashamed of,' he said. 'And there is no privacy in the clinics. You must go and sit in the public waiting room to be tested, and when you go to get your pills, everyone sees you are going to the clinic, and you are ashamed. And then for the rest of your life you must take these terrible pills twice every day which only remind you that your blood is dirty and that it will never be clean, that every time you cough you need to worry that you are getting pneumonia, that every time you wake up with a headache you must wonder whether the virus has gotten into your brain.'

For the duration of our research, Sizwe kept taking

me to traditional healers who claimed they could cure AIDS. He desperately wanted a cure, rather than a life-long treatment, and he wanted it to issue from age-old Mpondo wisdom. He would not test for HIV, he told me, until he found a cure. And every time we saw evidence that an ostensible cure had failed, he would close up and grow silent; he regarded the news as a defeat for his cultural pedigree, a victory for mine. He perceived AIDS as a racial attack and its treatment as a ceremony of collective racial humiliation.

What does this have to do with the fact that men are vastly under-represented among those on treatment? Is the connection between AIDS and racial humiliation an exclusively masculine preoccupation? Of course not, but men experience AIDS in particular ways. HIV is not only carried in the blood, but in the semen too. It is thus an attack on a man's capacity to sire children who will bear his name. It is an attack on one's permanence. It is to say that in spreading one's seed one is spreading contagion, that in the act of procreation and in the expression of one's potency one is spreading death. Bloodlines are masculine issues: they are at the heart of patriarchy.

Treatment practitioners have been shy to confront this nexus between masculinity, race and humiliation, largely because the vicious controversies over ARVs have made it dangerous territory, territory on which one might concede too much to one's foes. But it is a question that ought to be addressed if South Africa is to absorb the difficult truth that nearly six million of us and counting will need drugs to stay alive.

Anthropology of low expectations

5 June 2007

There is a new book out on the politics of AIDS in South Africa that ought to be widely read. It is by the French anthropologist Didier Fassin, and is called *When Bodies Remember.*

The most remarkable feature of the book is its peculiar tone. Fassin is aligned to scientific orthodoxy: he does not doubt the viral aetiology of AIDS. And yet when he writes of those who share his orthodox position – treatment activists, medical doctors, opposition politicians – he does so with unconcealed irritation, and at times with scorn.

When he writes of President Thabo Mbeki, in contrast, and of his seduction by dissident scientists, Fassin becomes the anthropologist: empathetic, generous, eager to explain, quick to understand. Why this dichotomy? What is Fassin trying to tell the doctors and the treatment activists?

He wants them to see that they just don't get Mbeki, and that they thus fail to understand what AIDS means in South Africa. For Mbeki is no eccentric 'dissident', Fassin argues. He gives voice to an aggrieved and quintessentially African experience, one shared by millions.

The aspect of orthodox AIDS discourse that began to arouse Mbeki's scepticism, Fassin argues, was its amnesia: its fixation on the present, its blindness to the past. AIDS was presented as a phenomenon without history, as if there was nothing in Africa's recent past to learn about illness.

Yet the very concept of Africans and epidemics has a long history, of which Mbeki was acutely aware. Among them is the story of tuberculosis. At the turn of the last century it was decimating black southern Africans, while leaving whites largely unscathed. Why this was so remained a mystery to medical science. Some spoke of a hereditary weakness among blacks; others explained black vulnerability to the bacillus by an absence of previous contact with it. What nobody proffered, not for a long time at any rate, was that the colonial economy was killing black people; an industrial proletariat living in overcrowded quarters on poor diets was the ideal environment for tuberculosis to become endemic. Steeped in racial prejudice, orthodox medical scientists were blind to the fact that blacks were dying from white domination.

Another echo, this one not evoked by Fassin, but one that amply serves his purpose. In 1908, an article was published in *The Lancet* reporting that 80% of the Baganda people of Uganda were infected with syphilis, threatening the population with extinction. The author of the article, a British army doctor named Lambkin, accounted for the epidemic by arguing that Western culture had exposed Baganda women to a degree of freedom for which they were not ready. 'They were, in effect,' Lambkin wrote, 'merely female animals with strong passions, to whom

271

unrestricted opportunities for gratifying these passions were suddenly afforded.'

By the late 1920s, it was clear that Lambkin and other medical scientists of the early 1900s had made a terrible mistake. Techniques for diagnosing syphilis, it was learned, made it indistinguishable from yaws, a disease of poverty usually acquired in childhood.

Such, Fassin argues, is the history of Africans and epidemics that Mbeki knew. Against this backdrop, orthodox AIDS discourse could only have aroused his scepticism. Here was yet another discourse on Africans and illness that was silent about poverty, about political economy, about the modern environmental conditions that have been killing Africans for generations. Instead, like Lambkin, it argued that the problem was Africans' appetite for sex. For by insisting that the answer to the epidemic was sexual behaviour modification, orthodox AIDS discourse suggested that the epidemic was uniquely terrible in Africa because sexual appetite was uniquely voracious here.

Thus, Fassin argues, when Mbeki got wind of scientists who argued that poverty, rather than a virus, was destroying the immune systems of Africans, his ears were open.

AIDS orthodoxy, Fassin argues, is the discourse of the victorious. They are blind to the past, for they have no bones to pick there. Mbeki, in contrast, is a spokesperson of the vanquished. They are steeped in history, precisely because it has not been on their side. 'There are things one does not forget,' Fassin writes.

The vanquished live with the past and feel resentment. Of the present they are suspicious, for they fear it will serve up more of the same. If, in his resentment and his suspicion, Mbeki got the aetiology of AIDS wrong, he also caught sight of some truths to which the victorious are utterly blind: about the racism stitched into the heart of orthodoxy, about the hurt of a people whose physical frailty and economic exploitation are inextricably bound. Such is Fassin's contribution.

As I read his book, I grew increasingly uncomfortable. I could not forget that Fassin himself was aligned with orthodoxy, and thus believed Mbeki to have made a terrible mistake about a great epidemic. What does it mean to write so generous and forgiving an anthropology of so large a mistake? What is it one ends up saying about the one who is mistaken?

Reading Fassin, a fictitious character kept coming to mind: Lucy Lurie, the white woman raped by a black man in JM Coetzee's novel, *Disgrace.* Lucy comes to see the attack on her as a kind of historical reparation. 'What if *that* is the price one has to pay for staying on?' she asks. 'Perhaps that is how they look at it; perhaps that is how I should look at it too ... Why should I be allowed to live here without paying?'

What Coetzee is conveying, of course, is Lucy's subtle racism. She is resigned to black vengeance because she believes that vengeance is all black people are capable of expressing. She is fatalistic about the future because her expectations of black-ruled South Africa are terribly low. Trying desperately to understand her attacker, she condemns him.

I wonder if there isn't something of Lucy Lurie in Fassin's book on AIDS. I wonder whether, in his ostensible generosity, he ends up condemning African politics.

Fassin is quick to talk Mbeki up as the voice of a resonant African experience and a powerful African nationalism. And yet in doing so, he comes close to saying that African nationalism was destined to get the aetiology of AIDS horribly wrong. Berating the orthodox for their blindness to the anguish of the vanquished, he is on the brink of saying that we must expect nothing more from African nationalism than resentment and suspicion.

Almost entirely unreflected in Fassin's book is the anger, the embarrassment and the sense of crisis felt in the ranks of the African National Congress circa 2001, the height of Mbeki's public talk on AIDS. Ultimately, Mbeki was forced to back down on this question by African nationalists; they challenged him because they found a future moulded in suspicion too pitiful to contemplate.

One hopes that history will come to judge Mbeki's AIDS dissidence as an aberration in the African nationalist project. For an African nationalism congenitally suspicious of foreign knowledge and technology beckons a future of low expectations, the sort to which Lucy Lurie resigned herself.

In the meantime, we should beware generous anthropologies of African mistakes.

Minister throws a spanner into the works

12 March 2007

It has been said over and again that the messages Health Minister Manto Tshabalala-Msimang transmits about AIDS treatment are confusing and destructive. But little has been written on how, or indeed, whether at all, the minister's utterances affect specific AIDS treatment programmes on the ground. I have a story in this regard worth telling.

Sometime last year, an interview with Tshabalala-Msimang was broadcast on national radio. I was in Lusikisiki in the old Transkei at the time, and the interview enjoyed a large audience there. Tshabalala-Msimang said what she usually says about AIDS treatment: that antiretroviral (ARV) medicine is available at health institutions accredited to prescribe it, but that those who feel uncomfortable about the drugs should consult one of the many traditional healers the government has accredited. They, too, Tshabalala-Msimang said, can treat AIDS.

I spent the following morning with a healthcare worker employed at a government clinic in Lusikisiki, one that had been dispensing ARV medicine for three years. As we walked through her village towards the taxi rank, person after person stopped her to talk about the previous night's broadcast. Some joked that she and the health minister should fight it out in public. Others remonstrated with her. That woman is both a doctor and the minister of health, they said, and you are neither. So what is your story when you tell people they will die if they go to the healers instead of taking antiretrovirals (ARVs)? Some of those who remonstrated were genuinely angry; by the time we got to the taxi rank, my companion was rattled.

Making sense of these interactions requires some background. Three years ago, there was no AIDS treatment in the villages of Lusikisiki, and ordinary people's definitions of AIDS were very narrow indeed. It was accepted that a person had died of AIDS if she suffered from chronic diarrhoea, got very thin, and then died. But a person who contracted cryptococcal meningitis or AIDS dementia was said to have had a demon sent to him by an enemy. A person suffering from shingles – a common opportunistic infection triggered by immunodeficiency – was said to have had a witch's snake crawl over her skin while she slept. As with all witchcraft illnesses, people sought cures from diviners and herbalists.

When antiretroviral medicine arrived in the Lusikisiki clinics, nurses began treating these illnesses as opportunistic infections associated with AIDS. People reeled in shock. What they had thought was a surge in witchcraft they were now told was AIDS. Across the villages, ill people were watched with intense scrutiny. If a person began suffering from shingles, her treatment choices were monitored. Did she go to the clinic or a traditional healer? Did she get better, or did she die? Often, the evidence was inconclusive. One person would visit both and live. Another would visit both and die. But enough people had gone to the clinics and recovered their health for the old explanation to have been thrown into serious doubt. Whether brain and skin infections were caused by witchcraft or AIDS had become a subject of debate.

There are of course healers in Lusikisiki who insist that their patients have HIV tests and encourage them to use ARVs. But in my experience, they are in the minority. Most I have spoken to say that dementia, nervous disorders and chronic skin diseases are the work of demons. They attract clientele because for many people it is more comforting to believe that one has been bewitched than that one has AIDS. The shame lies with someone else, not with oneself. And the illness is not chronic and lifelong; it can be cured by ritual and treatment. In the minds of many villagers, healers and clinics represent two rival accounts of the causes of illness and its treatment.

The people who stopped my companion on the way to the taxi rank that morning last year had interpreted the health minister to be saying that the matter was still open to question. Experiment, they believed she had said. Sometimes these infections are caused by this, sometimes by that.

To an outsider this may seem a puzzling interpretation. But in context it is not. For three years, government healthcare workers had been broadcasting their message over and over again: these skin diseases could be opportunistic infections, they said. You must test for HIV. If you are positive, we will treat you with drugs, and if your immunity is low you will go onto ARVs. If you hide from these realities you will die.

The health minister appeared to be broadcasting a contradictory message, one that threw the wisdom of her own personnel into doubt. Some of Lusikisiki's health-care workers were angry with her that morning; they felt she was undermining their authority and setting back their work.

Walking backwards into the fray

20 November 2006

In the wake of the apparent sidelining of Health Minister Manto Tshabalala-Msimang, a standard refrain has emerged. Give or take a little, it goes like this: 'The government is now talking right about AIDS treatment. We have turned a corner. We are no longer an international embarrassment.'

The issuers of the standard refrain forget that the question of the moment is not whether we are embarrassed but whether we can give antiretroviral treatment to those who need it. Right now, the answer is massively uncertain. We require a good deal more than the sidelining of Tshabalala-Msimang. We need a dose of courage and a breadth of imagination the public health service has not shown in 12 years. The mother of all tests has just begun.

As things stand, the national antiretroviral rollout goes something like this: in any given district, the hospital is the first institution to be accredited to administer antiretroviral treatment. When its workload outstrips its capacity, it can, in some places, but by no means all, begin to 'down-refer' to the primary healthcare clinics around it, a messy process that confuses patient and staff alike. But the hospital remains the district or regional epicentre of the rollout.

It does not take much to see that this is back-to-front. I doubt whether in the history of medicine anyone has successfully fought a pervasive plague using hospitals as frontline institutions. When an epidemic is striking at every adult population in each settlement across the country, hospitals are too few and too far away to hold the frontline of a programme of universal access. Their place is in the rear, treating the critically ill.

The consequences are there to be seen across the country. Hospital-based treatment programmes quickly bottleneck, and the waiting lists of people in urgent need of drugs grow and grow. One does not need to try very hard to collect story after story of people who died waiting. And where there are no waiting lists, it is often not because the programme is working but because people are not coming for treatment; they are dying at home, usually after successive visits to lay-healers.

It needn't be this way. There are more than 3 000 primary healthcare clinics across the country. They are more numerous, more widely distributed and far closer to the ground than hospitals. Doctors, nurses, managers, infrastructure, and, of course, drugs, ought to be diverted to them. They are, with little doubt, the most appropriate frontline institutions in the quest to treat South Africans with AIDS.

Why, then, are they being underutilised? The stock answer, it seems, has to do with standards and with race. We refuse, various government officials have said over time, to hand drugs out to poor black people as if they were sweets. Such like would surely not happen in Europe. If we are to roll out drugs, we will observe the highest standards of treatment, where patients are properly diagnosed and monitored, where the necessary laboratory work is of the highest order, where toxicity and resistance are guarded against with the greatest vigilance. If this means doing it slowly, and through hospitals, then so be it.

The tragedy of this argument is that it speaks powerfully against, not for, placing hospitals in the frontline. The average patient who presents at a hospital for treatment has come from some distance away, usually at great expense. She is counselled and briefed, she is given a supply of pills which she slips into her bag, and then she vanishes. The personnel who treat her hope to God that she takes her pills and comes back the following month. She is like a message in a bottle cast into the ocean.

Roll out through the clinics, and the patient lives perhaps 500 yards from the nearest community health worker, perhaps two kilometres from the head nurse. Everyone knows her name. If she has acute side effects, it will be known. If she stops adhering to her treatment and does not turn up for her next batch of pills, clinic lay-workers will find her.

In the area I know best, Lusikisiki in the Eastern Cape, there is a fully-fledged clinic-based treatment programme alongside a hospital-based programme. At the clinics, 2% of patients are lost to follow-up after a year on treatment. At the hospital, 19% are lost to follow-up. In the matter of rolling out antiretroviral treatment the hospital is without doubt the inferior institution.

So what is holding back government from implementing

the right model? One possible answer is fear: fear of institutional reform, and an inability to imagine it working. The last 12 years have seen incessant relays of institutional redesign, the largest, most difficult, and perhaps the least successful being the separation of clinics from hospitals and the placement of the former under district management. It could be that the government simply doesn't trust the primary healthcare institutions it has sweated over for so long. It fears that if it channels significant numbers of doctors, nurses and infrastructure into the clinics, they will vanish into a black hole. Which is really a way of saying that government feels fainthearted in the face of this epidemic, that it does not trust itself.

There is another possible explanation. Perhaps the fear of two standards, one for rich Europeans, another for poor Africans, really is animating the hospital-centred rollout. Perhaps the spectacle of a treatment programme administered at clinics, not hospitals, in villages, not towns, by nurses and cohorts of lay-people, and not specialists, is, in a fraught and complicated way, a source of embarrassment. Perhaps it conjures an image of African medicine as second-rate.

Perhaps, in the recesses that house our inherited prejudices, the idea of treating African patients with dignity is coupled indelibly to that of high-technology, curative medicine. The image is of a patient surrounded by machines and technicians and a battery of lab staff. That is, after all, the sort of medicine whites enjoyed under apartheid, so that is surely what should be extended to all.

If that is what is holding back a concerted rollout, the irony is sad indeed. Were western Europe faced with an epidemic of the scale we are facing here, would its govern-ments dare treat its people the way we are treating ours? Would it have its citizens die while awaiting treatment on the grounds that the highest protocols must be observed? Would it fail to bring treatment to remote villages because they do not have appropriate medical institutions?

It is possible that South Africans are dying in large numbers because their government is suffering from an inferiority complex?

Will this complex be sidelined together with Tshabalala-Msimang? We shall soon see.

Steinberg's book about AIDS in Lusikisiki, Eastern Cape, will be pub-lished in March 2008.

283

Mbeki's anxieties around AIDS have damaged national psyche

6 November 2006

What with so much talk of a lame-duck presidency, we at times forget that Thabo Mbeki's influence has profoundly altered our country's landscape. I am thinking in particular of the changes Mbeki's handling of AIDS has effected upon South African national culture. I would argue that his influence in this regard has been far more destructive than we care to admit.

Until he stopped speaking of these matters, Mbeki's talk about AIDS was a mixture of ersatz science and sociology. The science was primarily about the social and organic factors that cause disease. The sociology was a treatise on the force of white racism and the ways in which it has corrupted scientific knowledge.

Yet these things may well shroud the heart of Mbeki's response to AIDS, which was neither scientific nor sociological, but profoundly political. As the historian John Iliffe writes in his recent book, *The African AIDS Epidemic*, the government's early resistance to antiretroviral treatment is perhaps best understood as 'an insecure regime's anxiety to maintain control over a situation perceived as threatening. The threat was that pressure from a coalition of HIV-positive people, AIDS activists, political opponents within and outside the ANC, pharmaceutical companies, and international opinion might oblige the government to undertake an antiretroviral programme that it could neither administer nor afford at current drug prices, at the expense of its authority, its health priorities, and its wider developmental programme.'

Mbeki always spoke opaquely about AIDS and antiretroviral treatment, and by the time his ideas found their way to provincial ANC centres, they had splintered into an assortment of shards. But all had in common the same frenzied anxiety about an erosion of authority, perhaps even of national sovereignty.

The other day I read over the minutes of a 2003 meeting between then Eastern Cape Health MEC Bevan Goqwana and an alliance of organisations running an antiretroviral treatment programme in his province. He ordered that treatment be suspended at once, and when the organisations refused, he exploded, likening their talk to the warmongering of UNITA's Jonas Savimbi.

If the MEC's outburst was a little mad, it nonetheless captures the tone of besiegement Mbeki was imparting: these medicines were cloaked in antipatriotic mischief; they had been brought to our shores by people bent on stealing something from us.

What Mbeki coaxed to the surface of South Africa's political culture was an anxious man's nationalism and a paranoid's nativism – both of which instinctively lash out at the arrival of technology and ideas from abroad.

A few weeks ago, I found myself in a house in Pondoland arguing about antiretroviral (ARV) medicine with two wise and elderly men.

'I do not trust these drugs because they are not ours,' one of them said. He picked up a mealie cob that had been lying on the plate in front of him. 'This is ours. If a clever African scientist made an AIDS remedy out of this, I would trust it.'

'But mealies are no more African than antiretrovirals,' I replied. 'Five generations ago, your forebears farmed sorghum. Foreigners brought mealies. You started to use them because they were more productive than sorghum and required less labour to farm. You borrowed something foreign because it was useful, and soon it became yours. It should be the same with ARVs.'

'You are just trying to be clever,' he snapped, waving the mealie cob dismissively. 'What I am saying is that one must be very careful before accepting the offerings of others.'

Perhaps I was trying to be clever, but I know I was right. I also know that if Mbeki had not treated the AIDS epidemic as a pernicious attack on our sovereignty launched from abroad, that old man would not have waved a mealie cob at me. I am not saying that Mbeki fabricated the old man's stubborn and unreasoned nativism. But he did draw it to the surface of South African life, giving it the shrill and belligerent voice to which we have become accustomed in recent years.

I also know that Mbeki knows I am right about the mealies. Read through a random selection of his speeches and you meet a man acutely aware that a successful society borrows more than it invents. He is as alive as any historian to the fact that everyone under the sun who has flourished has done so using the technology of others. He knows it is the confident who borrow, the weak who throw up the drawbridge and shutter the windows.

And yet he has made his own sense of besiegement a nation's sense of besiegement. In diffuse and unhappy ways, he has triggered a flurry of trench digging across large strata of South Africa. It is a troubling legacy to leave behind.

For poor mothers, moral outrage is often a helpless cry of despair

19 June 2006

Some time ago, I used this space to talk about a young health-care worker in the old Transkei whom I called Nomaswazi. She told me that she treats girls as young as 14 for sexually transmitted infections, and I asked her whether these girls were using sex to bring home food and to buy clothes.

'Yes,' she replied, 'but why do you use the word "they"? I am also a young woman from a poor home.'

And she told me her story: that she matriculated in 1997 and had a baby in 1998; that there was no prospect at all of finding a job in her home town; that she left her child with her mother and went to stay with her aunt in Umtata.

Her aunt was very determined that she get a job. 'She forced me out of the house every morning,' Nomaswazi told me, 'and I was not allowed to come back until late. She was very strong. But there were no jobs in Umtata either.'

On the streets of the old Bantustan capital, Nomaswazi bumped into an old high school friend whom she told about her predicament.

'My friend said: "Come, we will find you a job." She took me to stay with her in a new RDP area, and I found out what she meant by having a job. It meant having many boyfriends. It meant going to a place and meeting a man there, and having him buy you clothes and food for the few months your relationship lasted.'

'What did your aunt say?' I asked.

'My aunt said nothing, my mother too. They are poor. They do not know where the food will come from tomorrow. You arrive home with a packet full of meat. They cannot ask you where you got these things because you are helping them.'

I have not met Nomaswazi's aunt or mother, so I am perhaps to speak unfairly of them. But I have visited dozens of homes like theirs, and interviewed dozens of middle-aged women about their daughters and their nieces. Homes like Nomaswazi's are often characterised by a particularly severe pedigree of sexual morality. Unplanned pregnancies are greeted with seething rage. Sexually transmitted diseases are met with accusation and blame. And the blame is more often placed on young women than on men.

'The young girls are the ones carrying the disease because they are always going out, out, out.' I have lost count of the times I have heard those words from the mouth of a middle-aged woman.

Yet the very women who accuse their daughters of excessive sexual adventuring unquestioningly accept the packet of meat they receive; they shoo their nieces out of the house in the morning to 'work', knowing very well what 'work' may come to mean.

What is going on here? To call it hypocrisy would be so ungenerous as to miss the point entirely. What is going on, I think, is despair and panic.

I put this question to a particularly perspicacious doctor I met in the Transkei. 'I think this severe sexual morality you are talking about is like the starch a poor person puts on his shirt,' he told me. 'Everyone knows the shirt is old and worn, but you must put on the starch. It is very important that people see it, even though we can all see that it is only starch.'

It is an evocative metaphor. We know from ethnographies and sociologies written during earlier times that two generations ago most women in Transkei villages could expect to marry into a productive household. And those who left their husbands or never married could live secure lives in their paternal homesteads. The result is that while sexual exploration among the young was common, it was precisely that: exploration. It was not a source of income.

It would not do to idealise the past, but it is no good either to deny that things have changed. During the last 20 to 30 years, it has become increasingly common for young women in the old labour reservoirs to reach adulthood without access to jobs or to productive households. Men are their only access to income. The blurring of the line between love and financial transaction has been chiselled deeply into the structure of their lives. It has become endemic.

The mother who accepts a packet of meat from her daughter one day, but denounces her the next as a slut who goes out, out, out, is issuing a cry of awful despair. It is the cry of a woman who watches herself and her children living lives she has not chosen, does not like, and cannot change.

Tragic illusions in a village split over the treatment of HIV/AIDS

5 June 2006

On the coastal road between Port St Johns and Lusikisiki in the old Transkei there is a village of some 400 souls called Nomvalo. It is so small, its place in the region's politics so negligible, that few who do not know someone there have heard of it. It is, nonetheless, the site of an extraordinary battle over the meaning of antiretroviral (ARV) treatment, and thus constitutes a microcosm of a national drama.

A couple of years ago, two Nomvalo residents heard that the clinics of Lusikisiki, some 30 kilometres away, were treating AIDS patients with antiretrovirals (ARVs). They had already watched several villagers die of AIDS, and were curious about the new treatment. Both took up voluntary positions with an NGO as community health-care workers and, one by one, began taking Nomvalo's sick by taxi to the nearest Lusikisiki clinic. Two years later, about ten villagers are on ARVs.

In March this year, the two community health workers announced at a meeting at the chief's residence that a mobile voluntary testing unit from the nearest regional hospital would be coming to Nomvalo the following Saturday.

Professional nurses would administer the blood tests, while several of Nomvalo's ARV-takers, who had been trained as counsellors during the previous month, would perform the counselling that couples with the test. About 30 people, largely young women, turned up to test for HIV. In the context of a community of 400 people, the testing process was never going to be confidential. The whole village noted who went to be tested, and how long their post-test counselling lasted. The counsellors themselves were villagers and knew each of those they counselled by name, face, family history, and a good deal more.

By the following Wednesday, a battle had broken out in Nomvalo. On one side were counsellors/ARV-takers. On the other were six or seven young women who had tested HIV-positive a few days earlier. The young women were aggrieved. They would not go to a clinic to have their CD4 count taken, they said, and if ever they fell ill, they would never consent to taking ARVs. The drugs were dangerous, they said. If you took them, you would give birth to a deformed child, or go mad, or suffer an acute episode of epilepsy and die.

'But some of us have been on these drugs two years,' the ARV-takers retorted, 'and we are not only still alive: we are much healthier than we were before.'

'That is because you are concealing,' the sceptics replied. 'You are secretly going to herbalists and getting medicine to counter the poisons in the ARVs.'

The dispute is a public one. Most of the people I have spoken to in the village have taken a position on it. Those in the anti-ARV camp are attracted to a discourse that defends personal autonomy. 'The chief has said we must test and take pills because the government does not need people to be sick and lying down,' a middle-aged man told me. 'But who is the government to tell me what to do with my body? I am not a cow that must be dipped.'

Those in the pro-ARV camp tend to adopt a militant discourse of self-care. 'People who say the pills are poisonous are not being honest with themselves,' a woman told me. 'If you look closely at who they are you will see that they are people who drink heavily, people who are depressed, people who are struggling in their lives. They are scared to take the pills because they are scared they will fail to take hold of their lives, to stop smoking and drinking, to take care of themselves.'

The two groups of HIV-positive villagers have thus been stripped of their privacy. The state of their health is a vexed political question. A great many people are watching closely to see who among them falls ill and, indeed, who dies.

There is some irony here. Clinical research has shown beyond doubt that well-administered ARV treatment drastically cuts the mortality rate associated with AIDS. And yet, if all the people of Nomvalo have to go by is the empirical evidence embodied in the health of their neighbours, they may not see this for themselves. The young women who all tested positive one Saturday in March may be years away from getting sick. The ones on ARVs, in contrast, have all been ill, are all at various stages on a slow and uneven path to recovery, and are probably more likely to fall ill in the next while than those in whom the virus is still latent.

That the health of a few people is the subject of intense and ungenerous public scrutiny is unfortunate; that the evidence may lie is tragic.

AIDS and enmity: marked by death in the land of the living

30 January 2006

The darkest and ugliest things we do to one another – things that are truly poisonous down to their core – are the most difficult to understand because they are the most uncomfortable to confront. I am thinking in particular of some of the practices associated with HIV stigma: the turfing of sick people out onto the street; the confinement of the ill to dark rooms where they are not seen or heard; the demonisation of their children as beings unworthy of normal life.

One way to try to unlock the difficult secrets of stigma is to begin by recalling that, unless they have access to treatment, those with AIDS will die. For the people around them, they are the walking dead: that they will be gone tomorrow is as sure as the fact that they are here today.

Psychoanalytic theory long ago taught us that watching and experiencing another's death is very complicated indeed. There is certainly a great deal of grief and sadness, but these are coupled, unconsciously, with ignoble feelings such as triumph and vindication. After all, envy – the desire to destroy another's pleasure – is among our primordial vices, and finds its ultimate victory in death.

This sense of animosity towards, and estrangement from,

the dying and the dead, is often powerfully captured in literature. In his memoir *In My Father's Court*, Isaac Bashevis Singer observes a group of mourners walking through the streets of 1920s Warsaw. They are following the coffin of a man called Mordecai Meir. 'Their manner,' Singer writes, 'seems to say: "Mordecai Meir is Mordecai Meir, but we are we. He's a corpse, but we're alive. He's about to be buried, but we must pay our rent and our children's tuition. We no longer have anything in common."'

I recently got to know a young man I shall call Ayanda who lives in a Transkei village in which many have died from AIDS. Ayanda is the most prosperous person under the age of 30 in his village. A couple of years ago he exchanged the cattle he inherited from his father for a bakkie and makes a good living transporting supplies from the nearest service centre to the shebeens and spaza shops of his village. While he feeds six people on his income and still manages to save, the majority of his peers are unemployed and penniless.

Success courts its own trouble. Ayanda is not a paranoid person. His roots in his community are deep, his networks broad. He has a pretty sober sense of who and who not to trust. He nonetheless spends a great deal of time worrying about the envy his success has spawned. There are relatives who he believes have bewitched him and caused illness in members of his family. Some among his peers live in a twilight zone between lawfulness and criminality and he worries on the days he goes to bed with a lot of cash in the house.

Over the last decade, Ayanda has slept with several

women in his village, and he knows that two have fallen ill. Yet he refuses to test for HIV. Why not, I ask him? 'Because the counsellors who test you at the clinic also live in the village,' he replied. 'And they talk. There are no secrets here.'

'What would happen if people knew you were HIV positive?' I asked.

'I thought about that a lot,' he replied, 'but it is so hard to put into words. Your enemies would treat you like you are already dead, and many who you thought were your friends would become your enemies. My business would not last a month. Those who want to destroy it would be able to destroy it.'

I asked Ayanda many more questions – like how their knowledge of his HIV status would give his enemies the power to ruin his business – but he wasn't able to say much more. Yet perhaps the very ethereality of his thoughts expresses their insightfulness.

It is a truism that communities are composed of rival feelings of solidarity and envy. It is perhaps less trite to observe that the spectacle of dying and death is as much a stimulus to animosity as it is to kindness. What Ayanda knew, inchoately, in his gut, is that to be marked by an illness which is itself marked by death is to be stripped of the invisible layers of armour that provide protection from your neighbours' darkest thoughts about you.

There but for the grace of God goes Edwin Cameron

11 July 2005

In his book, *Witness to AIDS*, Edwin Cameron tells a ghastly story about Botswana. Knowing that up to a third of its population had HIV or AIDS, and that about 100 000 people were in urgent need of drugs, in 2001 Botswana's government began to offer free antiretroviral treatment to every citizen with AIDS. Yet by late 2003, only 15 000 people had appeared at public health facilities for free medication. Why?

'Stigma,' is Cameron's answer. 'People are too scared – too ashamed – to come forward and claim what their government is now affording them: ... the right to stay alive.' Indeed, he continues, 'in some horrifically constrained sense, they are "choosing" to die, rather than face the stigma of AIDS and find treatment.'

Later in the book, Cameron tells of his gardener, whom he gives the pseudonym 'Gladwell'. Gladwell is chronically ill. He says he has tuberculosis, and is on prescribed medication, but his condition deteriorates over time. Cameron asks him if he has had an HIV test. 'I have,' Gladwell replies. 'It was clear.' His health keeps declining, Cameron keeps urging him: he still says he is 'clear'.

Gladwell knows that Cameron himself is HIV positive, knows that antiretrovirals have saved Cameron's own life. He returns to his family in Zimbabwe. Five weeks later he is dead.

In retrospect, Cameron chastises himself: 'Although I thought that I was offering him help, and thereby the choice of living, in Gladwell's mind he had no choice. The stigma associated with AIDS left him no choice ...

'I should have made him an appointment with Dr Johnson ...' Cameron writes. 'I should have told him I was leaving for Dr Johnson in ten minutes. I should have told him he was free not to come. But I was going and I wanted him to come – I wanted him in the passenger seat of my car ... I should have told him that my doctor would diagnose and if necessary treat him if it was AIDS. And that I would help him deal with his fears and loneliness if it was.'

Cameron's identification with the now-dead Gladwell, and the debt he feels he owes him, is very striking indeed. For Cameron tells us that he too might have died of stigma and fear; he too lived for a long time with secret shame. There but for the grace of God, Cameron *was* Gladwell; his identification with his former employee is thick, complicated, and deeply personal.

Why do people die, not from a somatic disease, but from their relation to it? Why do people die of stigma and fear? It is a huge, perhaps an impossible, question, and Cameron can be forgiven for taking only a gentle stab at it. But *Witness to AIDS* is a book of advocacy, and Cameron does have a good deal to say about what this spectacle means for human agency and solidarity. People dying of stigma, he suggests, are no longer autonomous agents invested with the freedom to choose (except 'in some hor-rifically constrained sense'), for they have lost their con-nection to their most vital self-interest, that of staying alive. But that self-interest still exists, even if its bearer has lost sight of it, and it is thus incumbent upon us to substi-tute for it, to steer the sufferer to the choices he would have made had he been free to choose.

Cameron is not suggesting that we force-feed drugs to the ill. He is suggesting that at the global level of public health policy, we do what Cameron, at the micro level, imagined he ought to have done for Gladwell; to lead him, quite assertively, to the conditions of his own survival.

Cameron's imagined relationship with Gladwell also seems to serve as a model for the sort of human solidarity he is talking about. He is suggesting that we lend our own capacity to live to those dying of stigma, that the capacity to live is, in a sense, a resource to be shared.

It is a strongly communitarian, and indeed, a moder-ately illiberal, position. And it is striking for being made in South Africa, a country in which bonds of social solidarity, measured by such indicators as our rates of murder and incarceration, are alarmingly thin. Indeed, our national response to AIDS – ambivalent, anxious, wounded and aggressive – is another symptom of the frailty of the bonds that bind us.

Dealing as it does with life and death, Cameron's book is among the most substantial contributions to the con-cepts of national identity, community and solidarity we have had in 11 years.

Why talking about prison sex saves lives

16 May 2005

Late one night in mid-2003, two male prisoners at Zonderwater Maximum Prison were having consensual sex, as South African prisoners have been known to do for more than a century. They were doing so in the relative privacy of a makeshift enclosure created by attaching blankets to bedposts. Some time after midnight, the blankets screening them were ripped off the bedposts, and they were exposed. They were charged with, and found guilty of, breaking the prison's ban on sex. As punishment, they were denied secondary privileges, such as reading and leisure activities, for 30 days, suspended for six months.

In response to this incident, the Judicial Inspectorate of Prisons commissioned its national manager, Advocate Kamraj Anirudhra, to write a legal opinion on sex in prison. He argued that prohibiting sex was unconstitutional, primarily for two reasons. First, an old common law principle, which has been absorbed into constitutional law, states that prisoners retain all the rights of an ordinary citizen except those taken away as a necessary consequence of their incarceration. Sex between consenting men on the outside has been legal for some time now;

unless the prison authorities were to convince the courts that private consensual sex between two prisoners would threaten order, there is little legal basis for banning it.

Second, Anirudhra argued that banning sex violated prisoners' right to be held in conditions consistent with human dignity. Enforcing celibacy, he argued, 'would lead to depravity, emotional problems and predispose [a prisoner] to unacceptable behavioural problems.'

In March this year, Minister of Correctional Services Ngconde Balfour responded to Anirudhra's opinion with visible queasiness. He said he hadn't read the opinion but that 'you definitely forfeit some rights when you're arrested' presumably, in the minister's estimate, the right to sex being among them.

If Balfour persists in holding to this position he will have done himself a disservice on two counts: first, for being shortsighted; and second, for missing a golden opportunity.

Shortsighted because the ban on sex in prisons has been unenforceable for the last four generations, and there is little to suggest that things are going to change now. Read accounts of the oral history prison gangs have been transmitting from generation to generation and you will find that sex is the central issue of prison life. Prisoners have ploughed decades of storytelling and mythmaking into the task of making it intelligible and acceptable. Banning it is about as sensible as prohibiting prisoners from dreaming. The ban can be enforced with arbitrary inconsistency at best, and thus serves only to nourish corruption and blackmail.

The golden opportunity being missed is that of preventing a great many people from getting sick and dying, both in prison and out. As anyone involved in HIV prevention is aware, knowing that unsafe sex can kill does not prevent nearly enough people from having it. The reasons are difficult and complicated, but among them is that denial of mortality is deeply embedded in human culture. Whether we live the backwaters of the Eastern Cape or in inner-city Johannesburg, we are all quick to uncouple infection from death and to banish the latter from thought and from view.

History has generally shown that prevention campaigns have the best chance of changing sexual behaviour when death becomes visible. When terminally ill people cannot be hidden behind closed doors, when the very face of a community is visibly altered by decimation, the link between infection and death becomes too stark to deny.

Which makes prisons pretty unique. In jail, people get ill and suffer in public view. There is nowhere to hide. In 1995, 186 South African prisoners died of natural causes. By 2001 the figure was 1 169. And that underestimates the visibility of the epidemic behind bars since terminally ill prisoners are in general released and sent home to die. Prisoners became viscerally aware of the connection between sex and death before most South Africans; they have no choice but to watch the progression of illness from day to day.

When I did nine months of research at Pollsmoor prison a couple of years ago, prisoners' fear of HIV/AIDS was palpable and extraordinary. Gangsters talked a great deal about death with apparent nonchalance. But when discussion turned to HIV/AIDS most became mute. Their experience of HIV/AIDS betrayed their casual banter about death as bravado.

It seemed to me that conditions could not have been riper for turning this fear into genuine reflection: about safe sex, about treatment, about self-care. In these circumstances, keeping the prohibition on sex in prison, and thus burying it deeper underground, is tragically irresponsible.

THE COUNTRYSIDE

Why those who need democracy most are least equipped to use it

9 October 2006

Some months ago, a fieldworker from an orphan support organisation in an old Transkei village agreed to let me shadow her for a day.

I shall call her Siphokazi. She was in her late twenties, and her job was both grinding and modest: it was to find all the orphans living in her jurisdiction, to ensure that their guardians received child support grants, that they were going to school, and that they were not being physically abused.

One after another, the places we visited were dismal beyond description. Our first port of call was a one-room mud hut, the thatched roof torn and patched, the door frame rusted and without a door. Two large, emaciated dogs were tethered to a post, and the yard in front of the hut was strewn with dog turd.

An elderly man and woman sat on chairs out in the open. Three children, the oldest about 14, the youngest four or five, came out of the hut to greet us.

'This is a miserable place,' Siphokazi said as we made our way from the car, and her comment took in not just the physical state of the hut but also its isolation. For even by the old Transkei's backwater standards, it was in the middle of nowhere: nothing around it but veld and scrub, the nearest tarred roads, running water and electricity some 15 kilometres away, the nearest clinic and school even further.

The two older kids gathered their schoolbooks and brought them to Siphokazi, a timeworn ritual, it seemed. As she paged through them the old man and woman watched her with interest. He was the kids' grandfather; she was his sister. All five of them were living off his pension. The old woman had come to stay here when her husband kicked her out of his home. In her haste to leave, she had left her ID behind, and had thus lost access to her pension.

'Why are they not getting child support grants for the kids?' I asked.

'When you live out here,' Siphokazi replied, 'you cannot just get a grant. The social worker will visit at some point, perhaps later this year.'

'But surely your organisation can pay the taxi fare to take them to the welfare office in town,' I asked.

'We have tried that. They were sent home and told to wait for the social worker.'

At a loss for what else to say, I asked how the kids were doing in school.

'They are clever,' she replied. 'I have noticed that all orphans are clever.'

'Why do you think that is?'

'I have thought a lot about that. I think God intervenes to make up for their misfortune.'

I stared at her, first in disbelief, then in despair. If these three kids had come off a shelf of human souls, to be distributed at random into the world, they had found themselves on the proverbial rubbish heap: in the furthest corner of the remotest dumping ground of the most unequal society on the planet. No God could possibly have put them here.

And if a potential Einstein or Tolstoy does indeed reside in their native intelligence, nobody will ever know about it.

I wondered how Siphokazi's conception of things worked. Perhaps evil, or just cold indifference, distributes souls into the world. Perhaps God gets a look-in at the last second, giving the truly downtrodden that little bit extra.

On the drive home, I asked Siphokazi about herself. She said that she had matriculated a decade ago and had not found formal employment since.

'I have had two job offers in my life and it was clear that both involved sleeping with the boss. I said no. With this orphan work, I am a volunteer, I get paid a small stipend, but the work is meaningful, and the boss is an honest man.'

As she spoke, it became clear that her comment about the orphans' brains was as much about her life as theirs, and when, on the outskirts of town, she asked if we could stop to buy her weekly Lotto ticket, I was not at all surprised. For God and the Lotto ticket share the same function: they contort the world into a shape that appears to give the wretched a future.

I guess this is better, I thought to myself, than a poisonous envy of those who do have real futures. And it is better, too, than utter despair.

In any event, from the vantage point of my day with Siphokazi, it seemed that those who need democracy most are least equipped to use it; the poorest of the poor are too busy remoulding the world into tolerable shapes to demand much from those who govern them.

Baba Mdu in the driver's seat
... at a price

7 February 2005

Several years ago, a colleague and I travelled to a village in northern KwaZulu-Natal to visit a 78-year-old man called Baba Mdu. Neither of us had met him before. We were working on a project gathering oral histories of the Bambatha Rebellion of 1906. Someone had told us that Baba Mdu would be happy to assemble a gathering of elderly people to chat about their understanding of the rebellion.

It was a two-and-a-half-hour drive from Pietermaritzburg to Baba Mdu's village, and the further we got from Maritzburg the more potholed the road became. Roadside billboards disappeared. The countryside was wild and uncultivated. By the time we reached the outskirts of the village, it was clear that we were at the fringes of the South African economy. The infrastructure was so poor that delivering bread must have been a herculean task. Thriving commerce was light years away.

We arrived at Baba Mdu's place to find him in a vest and shorts lovingly washing a magnificent black Mercedes-Benz. The scene was so out of place we had to blink before taking it in.

311

The old man chatted with us for a while and then went inside to change, leaving a neighbour to keep us company. The neighbour caught us staring at the Mercedes and laughed.

'He's a crazy old man,' he said. 'For 35 years he was a chauffeur for a wealthy family in Durban. He got older and older, but he refused to retire. On his seventy-fifth birthday, his employers told him enough was enough. He had to go. As a retirement present they gave him the car.

'Now, it is his life. He cleans it every day. He fiddles with the engine once a week. On Sundays, he drives it across the district at ten kilometres per hour with the windows wound down and he puts his head out the window and talks to everyone on the side of the road.

'The problem is money. The man lives on a state pension. Just to fill his tank once a month is more than a quarter of his pension. Sometimes he fills it twice a month. Then there is maintenance. The car is old. I'm surprised he still has money to eat.'

The old man emerged from his house in a clean shirt and we all piled into his black Mercedes-Benz. He did indeed drive across the village at ten kilometres per hour with the window rolled down, chatting to everyone we passed on the side of the road.

He introduced us to a group of elderly people, and we spent much of the day listening to their accounts of what their parents and grandparents had told them about 1906. Driving away in the late afternoon on the potholed roads, my colleague, who had grown up in a village not unlike the one we were leaving, fulminated against the old man.

'Look at this wasteland,' he said. 'We need every healthy

young man in this place on a public works programme rebuilding this road. When the road is rebuilt, commerce can come here. Instead the government gives its grants to crazy old men who spend it on their Mercedes-Benzes. It's flushing money down the toilet.'

That is indeed among the oldest debates about social grants. Do you give the poor money and hope that they spend it well, or do you patronise them and force them to spend it on what you consider to be in their best interests?

The current expanded public works programme, for instance, comes down on the latter side of the debate. It gives poor people a bit of money on condition that they do manual labour and attend life skills and vocational courses. The idea is that they will only get paid on condition that they learn the habits of work.

In contrast to my colleague, I thought Baba Mdu's story the most powerful testimony I have ever witnessed to the argument that welfare beneficiaries should do with grants as they wish. A dozen development experts sitting around a table for a week could not have worked out the old man's best interests. None of them would have guessed that stretching his lifelong identity as a chauffeur into the present, and into what is left of his future, would be worth half his monthly pension.

They wouldn't have known because a human life is too eccentric, too irreducible, to second-guess. Only Baba Mdu knew how best to prepare Baba Mdu for his old age and his death. Nobody else could have imagined.

The tranquillity, the trees
and the quintessential nightmare

17 April 2004

For as long as there have been cities, the urban wealthy have built countryside retreats. The ancient Romans would flee to their villas on the southwestern Italian coast for the summer. The Venetians built private estates at the edges of the northern lakes. And in Russia, even seven decades of Communism did not destroy the venerable institution of the dacha; long after the Russian aristocracy was routed, senior Communist Party officials would spend the summer months in the country homes of their defeated class enemies.

In South Africa too, successful urban families aspire to claim a small piece of the rural idyll as their own. But here, there is sometimes a little twist to this universal story.

A few years ago, an acquaintance of mine bought a stark, blond farm on the western highveld. On his second or third weekend there, he stumbled upon a grave while walking through his land.

'What struck me,' he said, 'is that it was freshly tended. Somebody had been there recently and mourned. When I signed the title deed, I was told the land was uninhabited. Who were these people who buried their dead here? What were their claims to this land? I got cold shivers. I

314

felt I had just bought myself into a history I didn't begin to understand.'

A while later, another family I know bought a farm in northern KwaZulu-Natal. On a weekend visit to their new property, they discovered that a small patch of their land had been freshly ploughed. Throughout the summer, they watched the empty patch become a mealie field. One autumn weekend, the crops were gone. A clutch of mealies was waiting for them on their doorstep – a silent thank you for the use of their land.

As benign as their uninvited tenants may have seemed, they were unnerved anyhow, and hired a private investigator to find out with whom they were sharing their farm.

These disconcerting little blotches that spoil the pastoral canvas are symptomatic of an irony that tends to go unobserved. Urban bourgeois families acquire farms to retreat from the world, but they are in fact buying into the one arena of South African society where the wealthy have no choice but to engage with the miseries of the poor.

It is often said that the old paternalist relationship between black and white has adjusted to democracy remarkably well in the cities. Less often observed is that in the cities problems are easily displaced. The domestic worker brings her labour, not her traumas, to your house; the unemployed people in her family who subsist on her wage are largely invisible.

As for the masses of the urban unemployed, the legacy of apartheid planning keeps them largely out of sight. They are in the shack settlements on the periphery, in the townships, and in those parts of the city the rich do not frequent. The only reminder of their existence is the miserable soul begging for money at the traffic light.

On the farms, the boundaries between rich and poor are less easy to patrol. It is not just that many of the poor raise their children, bury their dead and plough their fields on white-owned land; that poor people claim their heritages in rich people's backyards. It is also that the countryside has become a dumping ground for much of South Africa's pathologies. It is, increasingly, home to the frail and the disabled, and to those among the young who have failed in the cities and been banished by desperation to their erstwhile rural homes.

These young people are a strange and tragic breed. Neither urban nor rural, no longer children but not proper adults, they live in South Africa's twilight zone, scavenging a living wherever they can. In the urban suburbs, they are invisible. In the countryside, they are drawn to white farms like pins to a magnet. It is where they will find a grandparent with a pension, an uncle with a job, a roof over their heads.

The result is that the age-old relationship between white landowner and black tenant – which was difficult even in its heyday – is now saddled with an impossible burden: that of containing and managing a traumatised surplus population.

Such is a fate well-off people in unequal societies design their cities, their homes and their lives to avoid. The suburban family that fails to exercise great care in choosing its little piece of the rural idyll brushes as close as it ever will with the quintessential bourgeois nightmare.

Cheek by jowl and utterly incomprehensible

3 March 2003

When the leaders of the Boeremag were tracked down and arrested last year, investigators came across a document describing how the organisation planned to take over South Africa. Among the institutions the plotters wanted to seize in the first stage of the coup were television and radio channels, power stations and abattoirs.

Why abattoirs?

The plotters wanted to trick blacks into abandoning the interior of the country for the east coast. So they planned to line all eastbound highways with raw meat. The blacks would follow the trail, the plotters believed, and once they were all in KwaZulu-Natal, the borders of the province would be closed.

Trapped in the eastern lowlands, they would be herded northwards, at gunpoint, into Mozambique.

Think about it. And once you have gotten over how staggeringly stupid the plotters were, think about it again. How on earth did a group of men, most of whom grew up in rural South Africa, cheek-by-jowl with black communities, learn so little about their fellow human beings during the course of their lives?

Before I began doing research in rural South Africa, I had this notion about the hinterland: black and white had shared the same space for generations, they shared a love of the land, they often spoke the same languages. So, while they might hate and betray each other, they must surely know each other – there must be a nuanced and intimate connection urban South Africans will never understand.

I soon found I was wrong. I know the Boeremag example is an extreme one, but there are countless others. In every district in the KwaZulu-Natal midlands I visited, very few black peasants and labourers knew the real names of white farmers. They would rechristen them with Zulu names, each describing its bearer's character.

Sometimes it would take half an hour to establish that the interviewee and I were talking about the same farmer.

'Jones? I've never heard of Jones.'

'But his family has owned Greendale since the 1850s.'

'Oh, you mean the grandson of Bebetu. Yes, of course, he's a cruel man.'

Needless to say, those farmers christened with benign names were generally left alone. Those given pejorative names battled to hold on to their cattle.

White farmers had no idea what their Zulu names were: some had no idea that they had Zulu names. One farmer in the southern midlands, whose Zulu nickname meant 'Stingy', told me, in all earnestness, that his cattle kept being stolen because a Durban-based syndicate, connected to one of the finest steakhouses in the city, targeted his stock for their tables.

The blacks I met knew as little about their employers as their employers knew about them.

I remember telling a group of men how difficult commercial farming was – that most of the whites in the area owed millions to the bank, that one more bad season and 'Stingy' would have to pack up and stay with his brother in Maritzburg. I was greeted with howls of laughter and told I was naive.

Why do so many people of the hinterland know so little about each other? From the white side, it may be about the necessity of amnesia.

A century ago, black and white farmers competed in the same markets. There was fierce competition over who was to feed towns like Maritzburg and Durban.

Perhaps whites need to forget that they only won this battle because successive governments stole black land on their behalf. Perhaps understanding their neighbours would mean understanding history, and they cannot afford to do that.

Whatever the roots of this mutual ignorance, it makes for dangerous and precarious politics.

When you don't know your neighbours, you begin to invent things about them; during times of transition and uncertainty, the inventions grow increasingly paranoid.

So, a farmer is murdered for the money in his safe, and word spreads through the white community that that activist who stood up on a platform last week, telling people to reclaim their land was behind it; that the provincial structures of the ANC have turned a blind eye because they themselves are not delivering; and so the conspiracy theory spreads.

And when farmers in a district form a new farm watch, or hire a new private security company, the local land reform activist swears on his mother's life that a plot to assassinate him has been hatched. I wonder how many people have died in the countryside because of rumour.

Census rumours grist
to farmers' mill – again

10 October 2002

History is always better than fiction. Even Tolstoy, the finest of the epic novelists, would have struggled to invent what happened last week, and its uncanny connection to an event of a century ago.

30 September 2002 was the deadline for the completion of an agricultural census conducted by Statistics South Africa. The intent of the exercise was innocent enough. Since the last agricultural census was conducted in 1993, the liberalisation of agricultural markets has turned South African farming inside out; information gathered a decade ago is useless.

But in the rumour-rich world of the South African countryside, that is not how things were understood. Across the breadth of the hinterland, white farmers advised each other to stay mum. 'Don't tell them about your turnover,' people whispered. 'Or how much you pay your workers or whether you still owe the bank. They will use the information to appropriate your land.'

By 30 September, 2 126 of South Africa's 60 000 commercial farmers had completed the census. The farming sector had, in essence, taken a collective decision to hoard information from its own government.

I don't know whether news of the census's failure has reached the peasant villages of the KwaZulu-Natal midlands. But if it has, you can bet that many an old man has spent the last few evenings chuckling. For there is another census that looms large in the memory of the midlands' black rural families. The story has been passed from generation to generation by word of mouth, and is thus marked by a host of poetic embellishments; but the kernel of the tale is demonstrably true.

In 1904, 98 years before this year's agricultural census, the colonial administration of Natal announced in a series of meetings with black chiefs its intention to conduct a census throughout the colony. The chiefs were suspicious. 'What are you going to do with our names?' some asked.

The administration reassured the chiefs that the exercise was a mundanely bureaucratic one, and Natal's black leaders reluctantly gave their consent.

Eighteen months later, the chiefs learned that their wariness had been quite justified. Colonial administrators announced the introduction of a poll tax, payable by all unmarried black men over the age of 18. The information gathered in the census would be used to enforce compliance. The purpose of the tax was transparent; to force young black men off communal land and into wage labour on white-owned farms.

The response of black Natal was one of rage. Rumours spread through the countryside that Dinizulu, the only living son of Cetshwayo, was organising a rebellion and that all blacks should slaughter their white pigs and goats. A handful of Young Turks assembled makeshift armies and began what is known today as the Bambatha Rebellion.

The rebellion was squashed in a matter of months, its leaders executed. The chieftaincies that harboured the rebels during the brief campaign had vast tracts of their land confiscated.

A couple of years ago, while conducting research in the southern midlands, I asked numerous people when their land had been stolen. 'When the whites came and took our names,' some replied.

The strange poetry of the connection between the events of last month and those of 1904 illuminates something important. In South Africa's mainstream – in the corridors of political power and in the discourse of the national media – 1994 is understood as the inauguration of a project to build a single nation.

Yet out in the margins of the new South Africa, in the farmhouses and the kraals, there are many who understand 1994 very differently. Those who refused to complete this year's census and some of those who chuckle when they remember the connection between 2002 and 1994, have something in common. Neither understands 1994 as the birth of a single nation. Both understand the coming of democracy as another episode in an age-old conflict; a conflict between black and white that is measured in centuries, a conflict in which government is either for you or against you.

The story is a salutary one because it reminds us that the nature of the world we began to build in 1994 will always be up for grabs. Thanks to wise leadership, we managed to create, in law and in politics, a constitutional democracy grounded on the idea of a single nationhood. That is a hard-earned prize that will have to be defended indefinitely. There are countervailing ideas of who we are and where we are going, nourished by memories too visceral to ever die, that must always be kept at bay.

Rural South Africa still a
dumping ground of the unwanted

29 August 2002

I want to break one of Peter Bruce's house rules and talk about somebody else's column; the discussion Ken Owen began last Monday is too important to vanish into the ether just yet.

'South Africans, unlike Zimbabweans, have mostly abandoned life on the farm,' Owen wrote. 'We are an urbanised society, with three-fifths of our people living now in burgeoning cities, each ringed with the shacks of the latest refugees in flight from the land.

'Our policies recognise none of this,' Owen continued. 'They are devised by sentimental urbanites who put houses in the wrong places, and spend fortunes taking electricity and telephones to nowhere.'

Owen is right. The hinterland is emptying, but it is doing so in strange and disturbing ways, throwing the countryside into a painful interregnum.

I recently spent a year researching and writing a book on the events surrounding the murder of a white farmer's son in the KwaZulu-Natal midlands. The white man was assassinated by a group of his father's black tenants after a long and dirty battle over a small piece of land.

There were nine tenant families on the farm. Only two had a real stake in the city: perennial jobs, a rented home. Yet it was precisely the two families with substantial urban lives that led the campaign against the white farmer. Why? Why did those with city lives fight so bitterly over a slither of the hinterland?

A few kilometres from the farm, a church mission was in the process of giving away its property to the families that had rented plots of land there during the course of the twentieth century.

'As soon as news of the impending property transfer spread,' an elderly mission priest told me, 'scores of old names and faces began to resurface. People who had migrated to KwaMashu and Clairmont decades ago came knocking on my door. They hadn't farmed for a generation, but they behaved as if their lives depended on owning a piece of a rural mission.'

These are just two of countless stories. Practically every member of the last two generations of peasants and farm workers has migrated to the cities in early adulthood, swearing that they would rather starve than work the land. Yet their life stories seldom turn out as they imagined. They keep coming back, again and again, throughout their adult lives, to the heritages they have disclaimed.

For the truth they soon discover is that urban South Africa treats newcomers from the hinterland like dirt. In the mid-twentieth century, industry absorbed unskilled migrants in their hundreds of thousands. Today, all but a lucky few find that they are sentenced to live their lives on the periphery of the metropolis, their homes tin shacks, their neighbours acquisitive and untrustworthy strangers, the wages they get when they do find work barely better than those of the countryside.

Many end up journeying back to their ancestral homes incessantly during the course of their failed adult lives. They are drifters, not yet properly urban, no longer properly rural, scavenging what they can from both the cities and the rural villages.

It is these people who scare the daylights out of the patriarchs of the countryside, both black and white. Ask ten farmers who they fear most and nine will tell you it is the sons of their faithful old labourers, people they call 'strangers', despite the fact that the 'stranger' learned to read and write at the local farm school.

As for the black patriarchs: 'When your grandson comes knocking at your door,' an old man of the midlands told me, 'you do not even have to greet him to know what he wants. He does not want to mind your cattle or harvest your mealies. He wants your monthly pension payout. And if you are wise, you will give him something, because if you don't he will steal your neighbour's pension and your family will be shamed.'

Owen is right. The drifters of early twenty-first-century South Africa must be given a stake in the city, not the countryside. They do not belong on the farms. They only come back because they have failed, and they bring the violence and the despair of failure with them.

The old patriarchs scan the horizon in the hope that one day soon they will no longer be greeted by the sight of their sons and daughters, returning empty-handed. The longer the city falters, the heavier the countryside's burden becomes. It has not the strength to survive as the dumping ground of the unwanted.